D0581830

BEDLINGTON TERRIERS
KW-219

# Bedlington Terriers
### Elinore W. Young

*Despite his remarkably ovine appearance, the Bedlington Terrier is all terrier—he is not the softy he seems to be.*

# Contents

**Title page:** *The Bedlington Terrier has a distinctive appearance that is second to none. Owner, Starcastle Kennels.*

**Photography:** *Isabelle Francais, Fritz Prenzel, Ron Reagan.*

**Drawings:** *Scott Boldt, Richard Crammer, Richard Davis, Andrew Prendimano, John R. Quinn, Alexandra Suchenko.*

Bedlington Terriers on pages 11, 13, 14, 15, 16, 17, 21, 25, 28, 29, 31, 33, 37, 44, 45, 48, 49, 56, 64 owned by Starcastle Kennels.

The text of this book is the result of the joint effort of the author and the editorial staff of T.F.H. Publications, Inc., which is the originator of all sections of the book except the chapters dealing with the history, character, breed standard, and grooming. Additionally, the portrayal of canine pet products in this book is for general instructive value only; the appearance of such products does not necessarily constitute an endorsement by the author, the publisher, or the owners of the dogs portrayed in this book.

Distributed in the UNITED STATES by T.F.H. Publications, Inc., One T.F.H. Plaza, Neptune City, NJ 07753; in CANADA to the Pet Trade by H & L Pet Supplies Inc., 27 Kingston Crescent, Kitchener, Ontario N2B 2T6; Rolf C. Hagen Ltd., 3225 Sartelon Street, Montreal 382 Quebec; in CANADA to the Book Trade by Macmillan of Canada (A Division of Canada Publishing Corporation), 164 Commander Boulevard, Agincourt, Ontario M1S 3C7; in ENGLAND by T.F.H. Publications, PO Box 15, Waterlooville PO7 6BQ; in AUSTRALIA AND THE SOUTH PACIFIC by T.F.H. (Australia) Pty. Ltd., Box 149, Brookvale 2100 N.S.W., Australia; in NEW ZEALAND by Ross Haines & Son, Ltd., 82 D Elizabeth Knox Place, Panmure, Auckland, New Zealand; in the PHILIPPINES by Bio-Research, 5 Lippay Street, San Lorenzo Village, Makati, Rizal; in SOUTH AFRICA by Multipet Pty. Ltd., P.O. Box 35347, Northway, 4065, South Africa. Published by T.F.H. Publications, Inc. Manufactured in the United States of America by T.F.H. Publications, Inc.

# Introducing the Bedlington Terrier

The average person's first sight of a Bedlington Terrier is usually a startling experience. No breed of dog looks quite like the remarkable Bedlington, but his singular, lamblike appearance is only one part of his individuality. In the modern world the Bedlington Terrier has special appeal to the dog lover who is seeking something new and unusual.

## APPEARANCE

The Bedlington is of a size to suit any environment. The standard of the breed indicates a height of 15 or 16 inches at the withers. This makes it possible for the Bedlington to fit into an apartment household with perfect ease, but he is still dog enough for any suburban or country home. The truth of this is seen in the many times members of the breed can be seen in many types of homes.

The Bedlington coat is a singular feature not found in any other breed in the terrier group. It may best be described as "thick and linty." It is of a non-shedding character and is easily kept up with regular grooming. The Bedlington does require trimming in order to conform to the breed's lamblike appearance. Trimming for the show ring should be done by someone who is familiar with the breed and with correct grooming procedure, but the determined owner can acquire the knack of trimming with a little patience, practice, and observation.

At one time the Bedlington had nowhere near the coat he carries at the present time. In fact, he had a mixed coat of hard and soft hairs not unlike that of his nearest canine relative, the Dandie Dinmont Terrier.

The Bedlington may be seen in a number of unusual and interesting colors. The most frequently seen colors are blue and liver, in that order of popularity, but he may also be sandy, blue-tan, liver-tan, or sandy-tan. His coloring is another pointer to his close relationship to the Dandie. This is particularly so in the case of blue or liver, which parallels the Dandie Dinmont colors of pepper or mustard. Bedlington puppies are born either black or very dark brown, depending on what the mature color will be. This puppy darkness clears quickly and, before his first birthday, the average Bedlington will either have reached his mature color or be very close to it.

The Bedlington's general conformation is closer to a Whippet than to any other

**Facing page:** *The personality of the Bedlington Terrier is apparent in the expression of this dog owned by Marcel Rancourt.*

*The modern Bedlington Terrier is not as temperamental as his earth-going forebears; he is much more tolerant and makes a wonderful pet.*

terrier. This is due to his coursing-dog quarters and roach back. The Bedlington's tail is also like that of a sighthound, but it is carried in an upward scimitarlike curve rather than between the rear legs.

## TEMPERAMENT

A typical terrier, the Bedlington is full of life and dash. In fact, the only thing lamblike about the breed is its appearance. The Bedlington's sturdy Northumbrian background was not conducive to encouraging a race of "softies," and the modern Bedlington is just as capable of handling himself as were his forebears, although he is more tractable than his early ancestors. Today the Bedlington enjoys an enviable reputation as an ideal companion. He is a perfect family dog and is equally cherished by all from toddlers to grandparents.

This singular canine gentleman is also one of the most alert of dog breeds. He is quick to advise whether a strange sound is a cause for investigation and will announce the presence of guests before they get near the doorbell. This is very important to the person living in a small dwelling where a large dog with a "hair-trigger" disposition would be a true hardship in return for the service he renders.

Bedlingtons have proven their adaptability for obedience training. Those that have been trained have often shown themselves to be apt students without any loss of true terrier "zip."

## HISTORY

The exact origin of the Bedlington or date of his origin cannot be definitely ascertained, but it is generally believed that he sprang forth at about the same time as the Dandie. This would put the beginnings of the breed at around the start of the 18th century.

Of similar obscurity is the combination of breeds that went into the making of the Bedlington. The body contours of the Bedlington point unmistakably to a relationship with a sighthound breed, probably the Whippet. This

*Bedlington Terrier owned by Desiree L. Williams and Douglas R. Lehr.*

assumption is given further credence by the fact that miners and nailers of Northumberland, early supporters of the breed, had a passion for sports of racing as well as those of drawing vermin. A dog that could course as well as draw rats was far more suited to the hard life of his owner than a dog that could do one job but not the other.

The Otter Hound and the Greyhound have also been named as possible forebears of the Bedlington; like the Whippet theory, this is something that can only be guessed at.

In addition to hound blood, the Bedlington probably harks back to some type of now-extinct otter terrier. This ancestor he shares with the Dandie. Old prints of Dandies and Bedlingtons show a striking similarity in the two breeds.

In the early days, the Bedlington was a particular favorite of gypsies and poachers in the vicinity of the Border, between Scotland and England. It was not uncommon for the countryfolk to hire these dogs out to members of the landed gentry of the district for the purpose of exterminating vermin in ponds and woods.

The Bedlington began his rise to a place of prominence among purebred dogs somewhere around the year 1820. It was then that Mr. Joseph Ainsley purchased, from W. Cowen, a dog named "Peachem." Bred to a bitch named "Phoebe," he sired a liver dog, "Piper." Piper, owned by James Anderson, was, in turn, bred to "Coates Phoebe," owned by Mr. Ainsley. From this mating came the beginning of the true Bedlington Terrier.

It was not until 1870 that the Bedlington entered the exhibition ring. This marked the beginning of a steady upward growth in the breed's stock. As dog shows developed, so did the Bedlington. The year 1877 saw the establishment of the Bedlington Terrier Club in England and by 1905 there were three specialty clubs in that country.

## THE BEDLINGTON IN THE UNITED STATES

The Bedlington has found many staunch friends in the United States since being recognized. They have brought him along in a healthy growth pattern but have not exploited him or sought to commercialize him. The result is a smart, upstanding terrier that demands his share of attention and respect in all dog circles and with all those who value a good companion.

The first Bedlington to be recorded in the American Kennel Club Stud Book was W.S. Jackson's "Ananias." Since that time the Bedlington has

*Head study of a Bedlington puppy.*

demanded his share of top exhibition wins, including the Best in Show at Westminster by Ch. Rock Ridge Night Rocket, owned by Mr. and Mrs. William A. Rockefeller. These wins put the breed in a position of posing a real threat in any company of show terriers.

In the widely acclaimed and lavishly illustrated *The Atlas of Dog Breeds of the World* (H-1091) and the larger, encyclopedic *The Canine Lexicon* (TS-175), the Bedlington Terrier as well as related breeds are discussed in insightful detail. All Bedlington Terrier owners need to acquire these important tomes in dog literature.

# Standard for the Bedlington Terrier

The Bedlington Terrier, like all other purebred dogs, is measured against a breed standard of perfection, a written description of what the ideal specimen should look like. Each dog-registering organization has its own set of standards, one for each breed of dog it recognizes; however, these standards may vary, in the way they are worded, from registry to registry and from country to country. The Bedlington Terrier is accepted in Great Britain and the United States; both the standards of the American Kennel Club (AKC) and the Kennel Club of Great Britain (KCGB) are presented here for the sake of information and comparison.

## AKC STANDARD FOR THE BEDLINGTON TERRIER

**General Appearance:** A graceful, lithe, well-balanced dog with no sign of coarseness, weakness or shelliness. In repose the expression is mild and gentle, not shy or nervous. Aroused, the dog is particularly alert and full of immense energy and courage. Noteworthy for endurance, Bedlingtons also gallop at great speed, as their body outline clearly shows.

**Head:** Narrow, but deep and rounded. Shorter in skull and longer in jaw. Covered with a profuse topknot which is lighter than the color of the body, highest at the crown, and tapering gradually to just back of the nose. There must be no stop and the unbroken line from crown to nose end reveals a slender head without cheekiness or snipiness. Lips are black in the blue and tans and brown in all other solid and bi-colors. **Eyes**—Almond-shaped, small, bright and well sunk with no tendency to tear or water. Set is oblique and fairly high on the head. Blues have dark eyes; blue and tans, less dark with amber lights; sandies, sandy and tans, light hazel; liver, liver and tans, slightly darker. Eye rims are black in the blues and blue and tans, and brown in all other solid and bi-colors. **Ears**—Triangular with rounded tips. Set on low and hanging flat to the cheek in front with a slight projection at the base. Point of greatest width approximately three inches. Ear tips reach the corners of the mouth. Thin and velvety in texture, covered with fine hair forming a small silky tassel at the tip. **Nose**—Nostrils large and well defined. Blues and blue and tans have black noses. Livers, liver and tans, sandies, sandy and tans have brown noses. **Jaws**—Long and tapering. Strong muzzle well

*The punk rock appearance of this Bedlington puppy—"mohawk" and all—will disappear shortly before his first birthday, when his proper Bedlington coat will come into full bloom.*

filled up with bone beneath the eye. Close-fitting lips, no flews.
**Teeth**—Large, strong and white. Level or scissors bite. Lower canines clasp the outer surface of the upper gum just in front of the upper canines. Upper premolars and molars lie outside those of the lower jaw.

**Neck and Shoulders:** Long, tapering neck with no throatiness, deep at the base and rising well up from the shoulders which are flat and sloping with no excessive musculature. The head is carried high.

**Body:** Muscular and markedly flexible. Chest deep. Flat-ribbed and deep through the brisket, which reaches to the elbows. Back has a good natural arch over the loin, creating a definite tuck-up of the underline. Body slightly greater in length than height. Well-muscled quarters are also fine and graceful.

**Legs and Feet:** Lithe and muscular. The hindlegs are longer than the forelegs, which are straight and wider apart at the chest than at the feet. Slight bend to pasterns which are long and sloping without weakness. Stifles well angulated. Hocks strong and well let down, turning neither in nor out. Long hare feet with thick, well-closed-up, smooth pads. Dewclaws should be removed.

**Coat:** A very distinctive mixture of hard and soft hair standing well out from the skin. Crisp to the touch but not wiry, having a tendency to curl, especially on the head and face. When in show, trim must not exceed one inch on body; hair on legs is slightly longer.

**Tail:** Set low, scimitar-shaped, thick at the root and tapering to a point which reaches the hock.

Not carried over the back or tight to the underbody.

**Color:** Blue, sandy, liver, blue and tan, sandy and tan, liver and tan. In bi-colors the tan markings are found on the legs, chest, under the tail, inside the hindquarters and over each eye. The topknots of all adults should be lighter than the body color. Patches of darker hair from an injury are not objectionable, as these are only temporary. Darker body pigmentation of all colors is

*The coat of the Bedlington is a mixture of hard and soft hair that stands well out from the skin.*

## Standard for the Bedlington Terrier

to be encouraged.

**Height:** The preferred Bedlington Terrier dog measures 16½ inches at the withers, the bitch 15½ inches. Under 16 inches or over 17½ inches for dogs and under 15 inches or over 16½ inches for bitches are serious faults. Only where comparative superiority of a specimen outside these ranges clearly justifies it, should greater latitude be taken.

**Weight:** To be proportionate to height within the range of 17 to 23 pounds.

**Gait:** Unique lightness of movement. Springy in the slower paces, not stilted or hackneyed. Must not cross, weave or paddle.

### KCGB STANDARD FOR THE BEDLINGTON TERRIER

**General Appearance:** A graceful, lithe, muscular dog, with no signs of either weakness or coarseness. Whole head pear-

*Bedlington Terrier being "stacked" or posed in the show ring. Stacking helps to enhance the dog's proper conformation.*

The "unbearable lightness of movement" is evident in the proper Bedlington Terrier gait.

or wedge-shaped, and expression in repose mild and gentle.

**Characteristics:** Spirited and game, full of confidence. An intelligent companion with strong sporting instincts.

**Temperament:** Good tempered, having an affectionate nature, dignified, not shy or nervous. Mild in repose but full of courage when roused.

**Head and Skull:** Skull narrow, but deep and rounded; covered with profuse silky top-knot which should be nearly white. Jaw long and tapering. There must be no "stop," the line from occiput to nose end straight and unbroken. Well filled up beneath eye. Close fitting lips, without flew. Nostrils large and well defined.

**Eyes:** Small, bright and deep set. Ideal eye has appearance of being triangular. Blues a dark eye; blue and tans have lighter eye with amber lights, livers and sandies a light hazel eye.

# Standard for the Bedlington Terrier

**Ears:** Moderately sized, filbert shaped, set on low, and hanging flat to cheek. Thin and velvety in texture; covered with short fine hair with fringe of whitish silky hair at tip.

**Mouth:** Teeth large and strong. Scissors bite, i.e., upper teeth closely overlapping the lower teeth and set square to the jaws.

**Neck:** Long and tapering, deep base with no tendency to throatiness. Springs well up from shoulders, and head carried rather high.

**Forequarters:** Forelegs straight, wider apart at chest than at feet. Pasterns long and slightly sloping without weakness. Shoulders flat and sloping.

**Body:** Muscular and markedly flexible. Chest deep and fairly broad. Flat ribbed, deep through brisket which reaches to elbow. Back has natural arch over loin creating a definite tuck-up of underline. Body slightly greater in length than height.

**Hindquarters:** Muscular and moderate length, arched loin with curved topline immediately above loins. Hindlegs have appearance of being longer than forelegs. Hocks strong and well let down, turning neither in nor out.

**Feet:** Long hare feet with thick and well closed-up pads.

**Tail:** Moderate length, thick at root, tapering to a point and gracefully curved. Set on low, never carried over back.

**Gait/Movement:** Capable of galloping at high speed and having appearance of being able to do so. Action very distinctive, rather mincing, light and springy in slower paces and slight roll when in full stride.

**Coat:** Very distinctive. Thick and linty, standing well out from skin, but not wiry. A distinct tendency to twist, particularly on head and face.

**Colour:** Blue, liver, or sandy with or without tan. Darker pigment to be encouraged. Blues and blue and tans must have black noses; liver and sandies must have brown noses.

**Size:** Height about 41 cm (16 inches) at withers. This allows for slight variation below in the case of a bitch and above in the case of a dog. Weight between 8.2–10.4 kg (18–23 pounds).

*Faults:* Any departure from the foregoing points should be considered a fault and the seriousness with which the fault should be regarded should be in exact proportion to its degree.

*Note:* Male animals should have two apparently normal testicles fully descended into the scrotum.

**Facing page:** *The body of the Bedlington Terrier is deceivingly muscular yet very flexible.*

# Grooming and Trimming

The singular appearance of the Bedlington is entirely dependent on the manner in which he is trimmed. The Bedlington's famous lamblike appearance is not hard to achieve with practice. The new owner is advised to seek the help of an experienced groomer in the beginning. Practice, in addition to studying pictures of well-trimmed animals, and watching others as they trim will eventually impart the desired skill.

Certain tools will be required to do the job right. Investing in the correct grooming articles at the outset will be more than repaid by the pride you will take in the finished results you will turn out.

An electric animal clipper or a hand clipper will be necessary. The blade should be fine. A chrome-plated medium terrier comb is required for grooming sessions as well as for use during trimming. The scissors are of the utmost importance. Get the best you can afford—you won't be sorry. (If you are left-handed, make sure you get left-handed scissors, as you won't be able to use a right-handed pair.) Always keep supplies of chalk, or another whitener, and coat dressing. In addition to these, keep a claw clipper handy.

## BATHING

Your Bedlington should be bathed before you start trimming. Satisfactory results cannot be achieved with a coat that is not spotlessly clean.

The best way to bathe a Bedlington is with a bath spray. In this way, there is no dirty water left to drain back into the dog's coat, and there is never any dirty water for him to stand in. The dog should have a non-skid mat to stand on during the bath. The water should only be lukewarm, or perhaps a little hotter. Dogs cannot stand water that is too hot, and cold water can give a dog a nasty chill.

Use only special dog shampoos. These products, available in your pet shop, are made for dogs and are much milder than human hair products. They do not irritate the eyes either, and for a Bedlington, this is most important as the head and topknot must be carefully and thoroughly washed.

Soap the dog all over and then rinse him thoroughly with clear water. When all the soap is taken out of the coat, rub a cream rinse solution into the coat and let it stand for a minute or two. Rinse this out thoroughly and you will be surprised at how this

**Facing page:** *The Bedlington Terrier requires some grooming, especially if he is to be shown in conformation. It is a good idea to take your dog to a professional the first few times.*

## Grooming and Trimming

will improve the coat and make it more workable.

Have two or three towels ready when you remove the dog from the tub. He will probably saturate the first towel completely and you will need the others to take out the rest of the moisture. If you have an electric hand-dryer, this will help greatly to speed up the drying time.

**TRIMMING**

When you are ready to trim, put the dog on a strong table of convenient height. It should have some sort of non-skid surface and be fitted with a grooming arm to hold the dog steady during the entire process.

When the dog is dry, comb him out thoroughly. Make sure all mats, knots and tangles have been removed. Don't forget to check between and under the toes for mats.

With the clippers, take off all the hair on the underjaw and the underside of the neck to a little above the breastbone. Also with

*Whether or not you choose to show your pet, it is wise to crate-train him starting at an early age. Crate-training will make travel much easier for both owner and dog alike.*

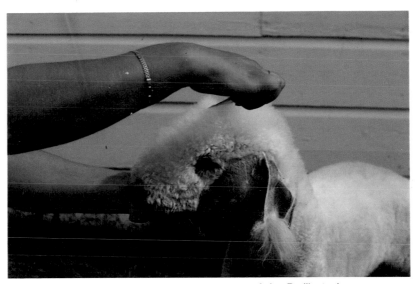

*The topknot is one of the most distinct aspects of the Bedlington's appearance. When working on the head—or anywhere for that matter—take your time.*

the clippers, remove the hair on the inside and outside of the ears, leaving enough hair for a tassel on the tip of the ear. This tassel should be about a half-inch to an inch in length and be diamond-shaped. It should start a little before the end of the ear. Straighten the edges of the ears with scissors, but be very careful not to cut or damage the double fold on the underside of the ear at the point where it bends. This can bleed profusely if harmed. The sides of the head should be clipped in a line extending from the nostril to the outer edge of the eye. The longer hair should be scissored so that it blends into the clippered hair.

The topknot should be shaped in a graceful Roman arc from the nose to the occiput. It should also be neatly shaped from ear to ear.

The finished effect of the head should be that of a blunt wedge. This will be heightened further by trimming the hair over the eyes into brows so that the effect is one of having well-sunk and triangular eyes as called for in the standard.

The neck should be trimmed to show a continuation of the line of the head. The sides of the neck should be scissored somewhat closer than the crest in order to blend into the shoulders.

The body coat should be about

# Grooming and Trimming

*Your local pet shop will stock all the grooming equipment you will need for a well-coiffed Bedlington.*

an inch in length with the hair a little shorter over the ribs in order to heighten the desirable flat-sided effect.

Trim the topline to accentuate the characteristic roach back. Start at the top of the withers and bring the hair up in a gradual unbroken line. It should reach peak height at the middle of the back and should then drop, just as gradually, to the tail. The upper part of the tail should be scissored for the first third of its length where it joins the body. It is very important to trim this hair so that it blends into the clippered tail. The sight of a "glob" of hair on the base of the tail is seen on too many Bedlingtons today, in the show

ring and out of it. The balance of the upper part of the tail, and all of the lower part, is clippered smooth.

The hair on the dog's rear should be carefully scissored to neatness. It is best not to use the clippers here. Take care when trimming around the reproductive organs.

On the hindlegs the hair should be blended where the legs join the body. The legs should be well covered with hair, but should be tidied. The inside of the legs should be more closely trimmed than the outside. On the feet the paws should be scissored to evenness. All hair should be removed from under and between the pads. If there are any stray tufts on the hocks, they should be taken off lest the dog be given an appearance of "cow-hocks."

Going back to the body coat, the hair should be clippered off the abdomen. To get the best effect here, have the dog in a standing position. The clippered portion should be brought back as far as the navel and the rest scissored to result in a shapely tuck-up. The hair on the loin should be trimmed to about a half-inch in length to further enhance a good tuck-up and deep brisket.

The front legs should be trimmed to straightness. Slightly more hair is permissible here than on the body. Any stray tufts on the elbows should be taken off, otherwise the dog will appear "out at the elbow." The feet should not appear round but should be trimmed to neatness, not overlooking the hair between and under the pads.

## REGULAR GROOMING

Routine grooming is best accomplished with the comb. The hair on the topline should be slightly teased to encourage the linty appearance of the coat.

The sides should be combed straight down to the tuck-up. Hair on the legs should be

*Regular combing helps create and maintain the linty appearance of the Bedlington Terrier's sheep-like coat.*

combed upward toward the body and then down. On the head, the topknot should be teased starting from the nose and back to the occiput. The tassels should be combed with the lay of the hair.

You will find that your dog can go for longer periods between baths if you make a practice of using a whitener and some coat dressing about once every week. Professional dog people usually use a fine grade of French white chalk. This is usually offered in the form of blocks and may be rubbed into the coat and then combed out again. For the show ring, it is imperative to remove any chalk or powder. Discovery of any powder in the coat, by a judge, can lead to disqualification.

Coat dressing can be either sprayed or sponged into the coat. When it dries it imparts an unsurpassed finish to the dog's coat. Many good brands are available, and your pet shop may have a selection from which you may choose.

If you can groom your Bedlington every day, well and good. If not, he should be groomed about three times a week. The time you spend in paying attention to your Bedlington Terrier's appearance is an investment in pride. This striking, beautiful breed that you have chosen as your companion will, with good grooming, reflect the thoughtfulness of his owner and the distinctions of this fine breed.

## GROOMING PROCEDURE

The following is a step-by-step grooming procedure used in professional salons. It may be a good idea to visit such a salon and watch the procedure used before performing it on your dog. Necessary tools and equipment for this process include:
- slicker brush
- mat-splitting comb
- medium metal comb
- A-5 clipper
- #15, #10, #4, and #5 blades
- eye drops (eye stain remover)
- medicated ear powder
- scissors
- toenail clipper

1. Brush the entire coat with the slicker brush, removing any mats with the mat-splitting comb.
2. Clean the ears using the medicated ear powder and lightly pluck any stray hair from the insides.
3. Clean the eyes by wiping with a cotton ball which has been moistened with eye drops. If the

**Facing page:** *A grooming table is a most useful item. Start training your pet to stand on the table at a young age; the younger the dog learns to tolerate grooming, the more he will grow to enjoy this necessary procedure.*

# Grooming and Trimming

eyes are excessively sticky and watering, with blunt-tipped scissors snip the stained hair from the corners of the eyes.

4. Cut the tips of the toenails with the toenail clipper, being careful not to cut the quick.

5. With the #15 blade on an A-5 clipper, shave the face, starting at the front edge of the ears straight to the outer corners of the eyes. From the outer corners of the eyes shave straight down to within one-half inch from the corners of the mouth. Next shave from the back edges (base) of the ears diagonally down to a point at the base of the throat, thus forming a "V" shape. (Note: When shaving the face, chin, and throat, shave against the grain of the hair.)

6. Shave the entire underjaw.

7. Shave the ears from the base to within one inch from the center of the edge and down both sides of the ear diagonally from the first point, making an

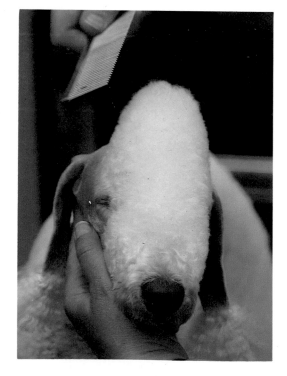

*Combing as you go, clip your dog's coat a little at a time. It is better to take off too little at first than to take off too much and spoil the entire appearance.*

Always blend the various trimmed areas into each other; this helps to create a more natural appearance.

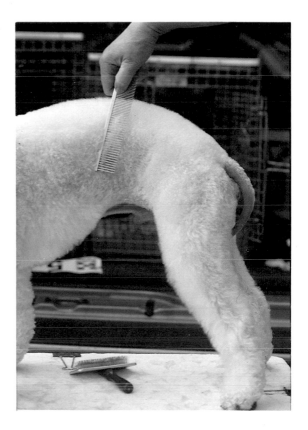

inverted "V" shape.

8. With the #10 blade shave the anal area, being certain not to put the blade in direct contact with the skin (one-half inch on each side).

9. Shave the stomach area from the groin to the navel and down the insides of the thighs.

10. With the #15 blade shave two-thirds of the tail from the tip, leaving one-third of the hair at the base. Shave the underside of the remaining one-third of the tail.

11. With the #4 or #5 blade on the clipper (according to the length of coat desired) start at the base of the ears and clip diagonally toward the center of the base of the neck, thus making a "V" from the base of the ears down into the neck. Then clip down the back to the base of the tail.

12. Clip down the sides of the

# Grooming and Trimming

*Artist's rendering of a Bedlington Terrier. Study photos of prize-winning Bedlingtons to get a better idea of the look you wish to create.*

neck to the shoulders and blend the hair down into the top of the front legs.

13. Clip down the chest to the breastbone.

14. From the first clip down the back, clip down the sides of the stomach.

15. Blend the hair from the top of the back on the rear end into the top of the thighs.

16. Brush through the hair on the legs, head, and face to remove any excess hair.

17. Put a cotton ball in each ear to prevent any water from entering the ear canal. Bathe the dog and towel dry.

18. Place the dog on the grooming table and fluff dry with the slicker brush, brushing the hair in an upward motion to make it full.

19. Using the same blade as before, repeat the process on the face and body.

20. Scissor the shaved edges of the ears, comb the tassels down, and scissor the lower edges into a curve.

21. Scissor the head into the Roman arc, i.e., arching from the

nose up and over the head and ending in a "V" on the neck. Scissor the sides to curve down and taper into the bases of the ears.

22. Scissor around the muzzle so that it is in proportion with the head. When viewed from the front, the head should appear long and straight, arching across the top between the ears, and tapering slightly on the muzzle.

23. Scissor the remaining one-third on the top of the tail into a tubular shape, blending into the body.

24. Scissor around the shave lines on the throat and stomach.

25. Trim the hair from between the pads of the feet and, while the dog is standing, scissor around the edges of the feet to give a round effect (doing this first will give you a guide for scissoring the legs).

26. Scissor the chest, between the legs and underneath the stomach.

27. Scissor the front legs into straight, tubular shapes.

28. Scissor the rear legs, following the natural contours. The insides should be straight to the hock joint and taper on up to the shave line.

29. Lightly comb through and fluff up the hair on the legs, head, muzzle, and tail, making sure they are even. Trim any stray hairs as necessary.

*After the entire clipping procedure is finished, comb the coat thoroughly and check for stray hairs.*

The Bedlington Terrier should be groomed every six to eight weeks. Regular brushing and combing by the owner between groomings will help prevent mats. The ears should be checked weekly and cleaned if necessary, and the toenails should be checked and cut during the grooming session.

*A pair of well-groomed Bedlingtons owned by Desiree L. Williams and Douglas R. Lehr.*

# Selecting Your Dog

Now that you have decided which dog breed suits your needs, your lifestyle, and your own temperament, there will be much to consider before you make your final purchase. Buying a puppy on impulse may only cause heartbreak later on; it makes better sense to put some real thought into your canine investment, especially since it is likely that he will share many happy years with you. Which individual will you choose as your adoring companion? Ask yourself some questions as you analyze your needs and preferences for a dog, read all that you can about your particular breed, and visit as many dog shows as possible. At the shows you will be surrounded by people who can give you all the details about the breed that you are interested in buying. Decide if you want a household pet, a dog for breeding, or a show dog. Would you prefer a male or female? Puppy or adult?

Ask the seller to help you with your decision. When you have settled on the dog you want, discuss with the seller the dog's temperament, the animal's positive and negative aspects, any health problems it might have, its feeding and grooming requirements, and whether the dog has been immunized. Reputable sellers will be willing to answer any questions you might have that pertain to the dog you have selected, and often they will make themselves available if you call for advice or if you encounter problems after you've made your purchase.

*Before purchasing your new Bedlington Terrier, decide whether you prefer a puppy or an older, more mature dog.*

33

A bit too big?
A little **too** small.
Too fuzzy for me!
Too fat to crawl.

Before you wrap it tight
And crate it home,
Behold its appetite
And room to roam.

A sloppy yap, a barking slur,
Puppy eyes to be let free,
A him? a her? an unmarked cur,
Let's pout to see its pedigree.

The perfect pet quest:
Which pup for me is best?

ANDREW DE PRISCO

35

Most breeders and sellers want to see their dogs placed in loving, responsible homes; they are careful about who buys their animals. So as the dog's new owner, prepare yourself for some interrogation from the from the person who sells you your pet.

## WHERE TO BUY

You can choose among several places to buy your dog. Many people think of their local pet shop as the first source for buying a puppy, and very often they're right; you should

*If you have even the faintest inkling that you will someday be interested in showing your Bedlington, be sure to purchase a show-quality dog, the best you can afford.*

remember, however, that a pet shop cannot possibly stock all breeds of dog. If your pet shop does not carry the type of dog you desire, there are other places to look. One is a kennel whose business is breeding show-quality dogs; such kennels may have extra pups for sale. Another source is the one-dog owner who wants to sell the puppies from an occasional litter to pay the expenses of his small-scale breeding operation. To find such kennels and part-time breeders and hobbyists, check the classified section of your local newspaper or look in your telephone directory.

Whichever source you choose, you can usually tell in a very short time whether the puppies will make healthy and happy pets. If they are clean, plump, and lively, they are probably in good health. Sometimes you will have the advantage of seeing the puppies' dam and perhaps their sire and other relatives. Remember that the mother, having just raised a demanding family, may not be looking her best; but if she is sturdy, friendly, and well-mannered, her puppies should be too. If you feel that something is lacking in the care or condition of the dogs, it is better to look elsewhere than to buy hastily and regret it afterward. Buy a healthy dog with a good disposition, one that has been properly socialized and

*A pair of Bedlingtons mellowing out for a while. If you would like your new pet to have a constant companion, consider getting another Bedlington at the same time.*

likes being around people.

If you cannot find the dog you want locally, write to the secretary of the national breed club or kennel club and ask for names of breeders near you or to whom you can write for information. Puppies are sometimes shipped, sight unseen, from reputable breeders. In these instances, pictures and pedigree information are usually sent beforehand to help you decide.

Breeders can supply you with further details and helpful guidance, if you require it. Many breed clubs provide a puppy referral service, so you may want to look into this before making your final decision.

## PET OR SHOW DOG

Conscientious breeders strive to maintain desirable qualities in their breed. At the same time, they are always working to improve on what they have already achieved, and they do this by referring to the breed standard of perfection. The standard describes the ideal dog, and those animals that come close to the ideal are generally selected as show

Owners of purebred dogs too often forget that all breeds of dog are interrelated. The ancient canine that is the believed ancestor of all dogs is known as Tomarctus. As packs traveled and inhabited various lands, types evolved through the process of adaptation. Later, as dogs and man joined forces, type became further diversified. This chart sketches one commonly accepted theory of the domesticated dog's development. Where does your dog fit in? With a few exceptions, dogs evolve or change as a result of a specific functional need.

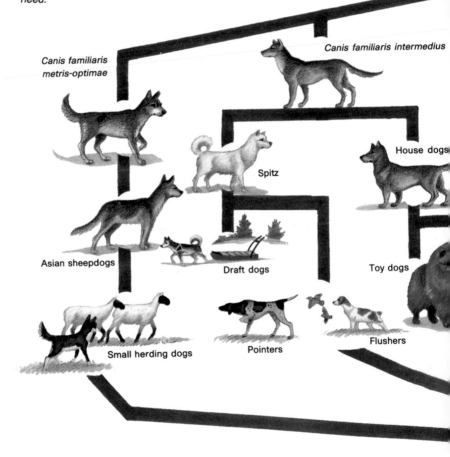

Canis familiaris intermedius

Canis familiaris metris-optimae

House dogs

Spitz

Asian sheepdogs

Draft dogs

Toy dogs

Small herding dogs

Pointers

Flushers

Tomarctus

*Canis familiaris leineri*

*Canis familiaris inostranzewi*

Russian Tracker

Molossian

Scenthounds

Sighthound
prototypes

Mastiffs

Sighthounds

Terriers

Bulldogs

Retrievers

Large herding dogs

# Selecting Your Dog

stock; those that do not are culled and sold as pets. Keep in mind that pet-quality purebred dogs are in no way less healthy or attractive than show-quality specimens. Sometimes these dogs even prove more hardy. It's just that the pet may have undesirable features (such as

*Part of the fun of acquiring a Bedlington is the gradual discovery of your new pet's likes and dislikes. If your dog enjoys munching on a quilt or two, immediate and firm training will discourage him.*

ears that are too large or eyes that are the wrong color for the breed) which would be faults in the show ring. Often these so-called "flaws" are detectable only by experienced breeders or show judges. Naturally the more perfect animal, in terms of its breed standard, will cost more—even though he seems almost identical to his pet-quality littermate.

If you think you may eventually want to show your dog or raise a litter of puppies, by all means buy the best you can afford. You will save expense and disappointment later on. However, if the puppy is strictly to be a pet for the children, or a companion for you, you can afford to look for a bargain. The pup that is not show material, or the older pup for which there is often less demand, or the grown dog that is not being used for breeding is occasionally available and offers opportunities to save money. Remember that your initial investment may be a bargain, but it takes good food and care—and plenty of both—to raise a healthy, vigorous puppy through to adulthood.

*Facing page: Head study of a Bedlington Terrier. Note the nobility inherent in this dog's expression.*

The price you pay for your dog is little compared to the love and devotion he will return over the many years he'll be with you. With proper care and affection, your pup should live to a ripe old age; thanks to modern veterinary science and improvements in canine nutrition, dogs today are better maintained and live longer. It is not uncommon to see dogs living well into their teens.

Generally speaking, small dogs live longer than big ones. With love and the proper care any dog will live to its optimum age. Many persons, however, opt for a particular breed because of its proven longevity. This, of course, is purely a personal decision.

## MALE OR FEMALE

Let us first disregard the usual generalizations and misconceptions applied to male vs. female dogs and consider the practical concerns. If you intend to show your new dog, a male will likely closer adhere to the

*Size variation in the dog family is extreme. The consideration of size must be a high priority when choosing a breed. The amount of housing, exercise, and food required, as well as the animal's lifespan are just some of the factors involved.*

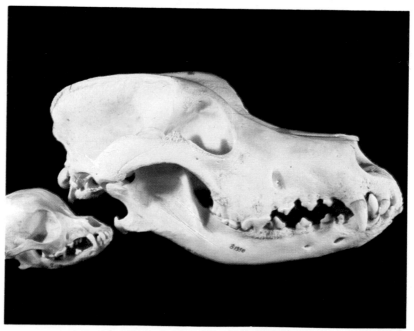

breed standard, though ring competition for males is stiffer. A female chosen to show cannot be spayed and the owner must contend with the bitch's heat period. If it is solely a pet—and pet animals should *not* be bred—castration or spaying is necessary. Neutered pets have longer lifespans and have a decreased risk of cancer. Males are more economical to neuter than are females. You might also consider that females are generally smaller than males, easier to housetrain, may be more family-oriented and protective of home and property. Any dog will roam—male or female—castration will not affect roaming in most cases. Males are larger and stronger, proving better guard-dog candidates. Of course, a dog of either sex, if properly trained, can make a charming, reliable, and loving pet. Male vs. female is chiefly a matter of personal preference—go with your first instinct.

## ADULT OR PUP

Whether to buy a grown dog or a young puppy is another question. It is surely an undeniable pleasure to watch your dog grow from a lively pup to a mature, dignified dog. If you don't have the time to spend on the more frequent meals, housebreaking, and other training a puppy needs in order to become a dog you can be

| Life Expectancy | |
| --- | --- |
| Dog's Age in Years | Comparative Human Age in Years |
| 1 | ......15 |
| 2 | ......24 |
| 3 | ......28 |
| 4 | ......32 |
| 5 | ......36 |
| 6 | ......40 |
| 7 | ......44 |
| 8 | ......48 |
| 9 | ......52 |
| 10 | ......56 |
| 11 | ......60 |
| 12 | ......64 |
| 13 | ......68 |
| 14 | ......72 |
| 15 | ......76 |
| 16 | ......80 |
| 17 | ......84 |
| 18 | ......88 |
| 19 | ......92 |
| 20 | ......96 |
| 21 | ......100 |

*This chart is designed to provide a comparative view of ages between a dog and its human counterpart. Necessarily it is an oversimplification since larger breeds often have shorter lifespans than do average or medium-sized dogs; likewise working dogs may tend to live shorter lives than the easygoing pet dog. These factors, and many others, must be taken into account when considering this chart.*

proud of, then choose an older, partly trained adolescent or a grown dog. If you want a show dog, remember that no one, not even an expert, can predict with one hundred percent accuracy what a puppy will be like when he grows up. The dog may seem to exhibit show potential *most* of the time, but six months is the earliest age for the would-be exhibitor to select a prospect and know that its future is in the show ring.

If you have a small child, it is best to get a puppy big enough to defend itself, one not less than four or five months old.

Older children will enjoy playing with and helping to take care of a baby pup; but at less than four months, a puppy wants to do little else but eat and sleep, and he must be protected from teasing and overtiring. You cannot expect a very young child to understand that a puppy is a fragile living being; to the youngster he is a toy like his

*Many Bedlingtons, especially puppies, love wrestling in the great outdoors—Greco-Scottish style, of course.*

A pair of mohawk puppies taking a break in their owner's lap.

stuffed dog. Children, therefore, must learn how to handle and care for their young pets.

We recommend that you start with a puppy so you can raise and train it according to the rules you have established in your own home. While a dog is young, its behavior can be more easily shaped by the owner, whereas an older dog, although trainable, may be a bit set in his ways.

## WHAT TO LOOK FOR IN A PUPPY

In choosing a puppy, assuming that it comes from healthy, well-bred parents, look for one that is friendly and outgoing. The biggest pup in the litter is apt to be somewhat coarse as a grown dog, while the appealing "runt of the litter" may turn out to be a timid shadow—or have a Napoleonic complex! If you want a show dog and have no experience in choosing a prospect, study the breed standard and listen carefully to the breeder on the finer points of show conformation. A breeder's prices will be in accord with his puppies' expected worth, and he will be honest with you about each pup's potential because it is to his own advantage. He wants his top-quality show puppies placed in the public eye to reflect glory on him—and to attract future buyers. Why should he sell a potential show champion to someone who just wants a pet?

Now that you have paid your money and made your choice, you are ready to depart with puppy, papers, and instructions. Make sure that you know the youngster's feeding routine, and take along some of his food. For the trip home, place him in a comfortable, sturdy carrier. Do not drive home with a puppy on your lap! If you'll be travelling for a few hours, at the very least bring along a bottle of water from the breeder and a small water dish.

## PEDIGREE AND REGISTRATION

Owners of puppies are often misled by sellers with such ruses as leading the owner to believe his dog is something special. The term *pedigree papers* is quite different from the term *registration papers*. A pedigree is nothing more than a statement made by the breeder of the dog;

*If you have never been to a dog show, whether you're interested in show dogs or not, by all means—Go! An all-breed dog show will give you hands-on experience with different breeds of dog, the chance to meet their owners and breeders, and the answers to many of your questions.*

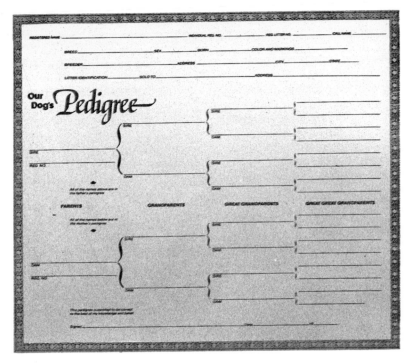

*Pedigree papers can trace a dog's lineage back several generations. They do not, however, guarantee that a puppy is purebred, healthy or sound.*

and it is written on special pedigree blanks, which are readily available from any pet shop or breed club, with the names of several generations from which the new puppy comes. It records your puppy's ancestry and other important data, such as the pup's date of birth, its breed, its sex, its sire and dam, its breeder's name and address, and so on. If your dog has had purebred champions in his background, then the pedigree papers are valuable as evidence of the good breeding behind your dog; but if the names on the pedigree paper are meaningless, then so is the paper itself. Just because a dog has a pedigree doesn't necessarily mean he is registered with a kennel club.

Registration papers from the American Kennel Club or the United Kennel Club in the United States or The Kennel Club of Great Britain attest to the fact that the mother and father of your puppy were purebred dogs of the breed represented by your puppy and that they were registered with a particular club. Normally every registered dog also has a complete pedigree available. Registration papers, which you receive when you buy a puppy, merely enable you to register your puppy. Usually the breeder has registered only the litter, so it is the new owner's responsibility to register and name an individual pup. The papers should be filled out and sent to the appropriate address printed on the application, along with the fee required for the registration. A certificate of registration will then be sent to you.

Pedigree and registration, by the way, have nothing to do with licensing, which is a local regulation applying to purebred and mongrel alike. Find out what the local ordinance is in your town or city and how it applies to your dog; then buy a license and keep it on your dog's collar for identification.

*Bedlington Terrier at a show. Note the typical arched loin, a by-product of the Bedlington's sighthound ancestry.*

# The New Family Member

*A pair of puppies inside their crate. Be sure to give your new pet plenty of space when he first comes home with you—let him adjust at his own pace.*

At long last, the day you have all been waiting for, your new puppy will make its grand entrance into your home. Before you bring your companion to his new residence, however, you must plan carefully for his arrival. Keep in mind that the puppy will need

# The New Family Member

time to adjust to life with a different owner. He may seem a bit apprehensive about the strange surroundings in which he finds himself, having spent the first few weeks of life with his dam and littermates, but in a couple of days, with love and patience on your part, the transition will be complete.

First impressions are important, especially from the puppy's point of view, and these may very well set the pattern of his future relationship with you. You must be consistent in the

*The puppy's bed will provide a place of refuge and privacy. Make sure that the puppy's toilet needs have been met before sending him to bed for the night.*

way you handle your pet so that he learns what is expected of him. He must come to trust and respect you as his keeper and master. Provide him with proper care and attention, and you will be rewarded with a loyal companion for many years. Considering the needs of your puppy and planning ahead will surely make the change from his former home to his new one easier.

## ADVANCE PREPARATION

In preparing for your puppy's arrival, perhaps more important than anything else is to find out from the seller how the pup was maintained. What brand of food was offered and when and how often was the puppy fed? Has

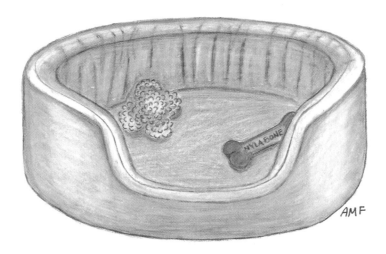

## BASIC PUPPY NEEDS

- Canned and dry food/diet schedule
- Feeding and water bowls
- Carrying/sleeping crate
- Bed
- Collar and leash
- Grooming supplies (brushes, shampoo, etc.)
- Outdoor lead and/or pen
- Muzzle/first-aid kit
- Flea collar and preparations
- Safe chew products (Nylabone®, Gumabone®)
- Edible chew products (treats/rewards)

the pup been housebroken; if so, what method was employed? Attempt to continue whatever routine was started by the person from whom you bought your puppy; then, gradually, you can make those changes that suit you and your lifestyle. If, for example, the puppy has been paper trained, plan to stock up on newspaper. Place this newspaper toilet facility in a selected spot so that your puppy learns to use the designated area as his "bathroom." And keep on hand a supply of the dog food to which he is accustomed, as a sudden switch to new food could cause digestive upsets.

Another consideration is sleeping and resting quarters. Be sure to supply a dog bed for your pup, and introduce him to his special cozy corner so that he

*This chart lists some of the many items that the dog owner should have on hand before he brings home his new charge.*

knows where to retire when he feels like taking a snooze. You'll need to buy a collar (or harness) and leash, a safe chew item (such as Nylabone® or Gumabone®), and a few grooming tools as well. A couple of sturdy feeding dishes, one for food and one for water, will be needed; and it will be necessary, beforehand, to set up a feeding station.

### FINDING A VETERINARIAN

An important part of your preparations should include finding a local veterinarian who can provide quality health care in the form of routine check-ups, inoculations, and prompt medical attention in case of illness or emergency. Find out if the animal you have selected has been vaccinated against canine diseases, and make certain you secure all health certificates at the time of purchase. This information will be valuable to your veterinarian, who will want to know the puppy's complete medical history. Incidentally, don't wait until your puppy becomes sick before you seek the services of a vet; make an appointment for your pup before or soon after he takes up residence with you so that he starts out with a clean bill of health in his new home.

## CHILDREN AND PUPPIES

Instruct the young members of the household on pet care. Children should learn not only to love their charges but to respect them and treat them with the consideration that one would give all living things. It must be emphasized to youngsters that the puppy has certain needs, just as humans have, and all family members must take an active role in ensuring that these needs are met. Someone must feed the puppy. Someone must walk him a couple of times a day or clean up after him if he is trained to relieve himself on newspaper. Someone must groom his coat, clean his ears, and clip his nails from time to time. Someone,

must see to it that the puppy gets sufficient exercise and attention each day.

A child who has a pet to care for learns responsibility; nonetheless, parental guidance is an essential part of this learning experience. Many a child has been known to "love a pet to death," squeezing and hugging the animal in ways which are irritating or even painful. Others have been found guilty of teasing, perhaps unintentionally, and disturbing their pet while the animal is eating or resting. One must teach a child, therefore, when and how to stroke and fondle a puppy gently. In time, the child can learn how to pick up and handle the pup with care. A dog should always be supported with both hands, *not* lifted by the scruff of the neck. One hand placed under the chest, between the front legs, and the other hand supporting the dog's rear end will be comfortable and will restrain the animal as you hold and carry it. Always demonstrate to children the proper way to lift a dog.

## BE A GOOD NEIGHBOR

For the sake of your dog's safety and well being, don't allow him to wander onto the property of others. Keep him confined at all times to your own yard or indoors where he won't become a nuisance. Consider what

The Bedlington Terrier makes an ideal pet if he is treated with the kindness and consideration all living things deserve.

Clockwise from upper right: *pokeweed, jimson weed, foxglove, and yew.* If ingested, any toxic plant can be dangerous to your dog.

Rover will not be Harmed if you follow My instructions

AMF

*Dog theft is not an uncommon event. Dognappers will steal either a purebred or mongrel puppy so all owners must always be wary.*

dangers lie ahead for an unleashed dog that has total freedom of the great outdoors, particularly when he is unsupervised by his master. There are cars and trucks to dodge on the streets and highways. There are stray animals with which to wrangle. There are poisons all around, such as car antifreeze in driveways or toxic plants and shrubs, which, if swallowed, could prove fatal. There are dognappers and sadistic people who may steal or bring harm to your beloved pet. In short, there are all sorts of nasty things waiting to hurt him. Did you know that if your dog consumes rotting garbage, there is the possibility he could go into shock or even die? And are you aware that a dog left to roam in a wooded area or field could become infected with any number of parasites if he plays with or ingests some small prey, such as a rabbit, that might be carrying these parasitic organisms? A thorn from a rosebush imbedded in the dog's foot pad, tar from a newly paved road stuck to his coat, and a wound inflicted by a wild animal all can be avoided if you take the precaution of keeping your dog in a safe enclosure where he will be protected from such dangers. Don't let your dog run loose; he is likely to stray from home and get into all sorts of trouble.

# The New Family Member

## GETTING ACQUAINTED

Plan to bring your new pet home in the morning so that by nightfall he will have had some time to become acquainted with you and his new environment. Avoid introducing the pup to the family around holiday time, since the extra excitement will only add to the confusion and frighten him. Let the puppy enter your home on a day when the routine

Resist the temptation to handle him too much during these first few days. And, if there are other dogs or animals around the house, make certain that all are properly introduced. If you observe fighting among the animals, or some other problem, you may have to separate all parties until they learn to accept one another. Remember that neglecting your other pets while

is normal. For those people who work during the week, a Saturday morning is an ideal time to bring the puppy to his new home. Let the puppy explore, under your watchful eye, of course, and let him come to know his new home without stress and fear.

*If your Bedlington is to be introduced to other pets, be present at their first few encounters to ensure that the animals learn to accept each other.*

**Facing page:** *The more time you spend with your new Bedlington, the closer the two of you will become.*

showering the new puppy with extra attention will only cause animosity and jealousy. Make an effort to pay special attention to the other animals as well.

On that eventful first night, try not to give in and let the puppy sleep with you; otherwise, this could become a difficult habit to break. Let him cry and whimper, even if it means a night of restlessness for the entire family. Some people have had success with putting a doll or a hot water bottle wrapped in a towel in the puppy's bed as a surrogate mother, while others have placed a ticking alarm clock in the bed to simulate the heartbeat of the pup's dam and littermates. Remember that this furry little fellow is used to the warmth and security of his mother and siblings, so the adjustment to sleeping alone will take time. Select a location away from drafts and away from the feeding station for placement of his dog bed. Keep in mind, also, that the bed should be roomy enough for him to stretch out in; as he grows older, you may need to supply a larger one.

Prior to the pup's arrival, set up his room and partition it the way you would to keep an infant out of a particular area. You may want to keep his bed, his feeding station, and his toilet area all in the same room—in separate locations—or you may want to set the feeding station up in your kitchen, where meals for all family members are served. Whatever you decide, do it ahead of time so you will have that much less to worry about when your puppy finally moves in with you.

Above all else, be patient with your puppy as he adjusts to life in his new home. If you purchase a pup that is not housebroken, you will have to spend time with the dog—just as you would with a small child—until he develops proper toilet habits. Even a housebroken puppy may feel nervous in strange new surroundings and have an occasional accident. Praise and encouragement will elicit far better results than punishment or scolding. Remember that your puppy wants nothing more than to please you, thus he is anxious to learn the behavior that is required of him.

# Feeding Requirements

Perhaps more than any other single aspect of your dog's development, proper feeding requires an educated and responsible dog owner. The importance of nutrition on your dog's bone and muscle growth cannot be overemphasized. Soon after your puppy comes to live with you, he will need to be fed. Remember to ask the seller what foods were given to the youngster and stay with that diet for a while. It is important for the puppy to keep eating and to avoid skipping a meal, so entice him with the food to which he is accustomed. If you prefer to switch to some other brand of dog food, each day begin to add small quantities of the new brand to the usual food offering. Make the portions of the new food progressively larger until the pup is weaned from his former diet.

What should you feed the puppy and how often? His diet is really quite simple and relatively inexpensive to prepare. Puppies need to be fed small portions at frequent intervals, since they are growing and their activity level is high. You must ensure that your pup gains weight steadily; with an adult dog, however, growth slows down and weight must be regulated to prevent obesity and a host of other problems. At one time, it was thought that home-cooked meals were the answer, with daily rations of meat,

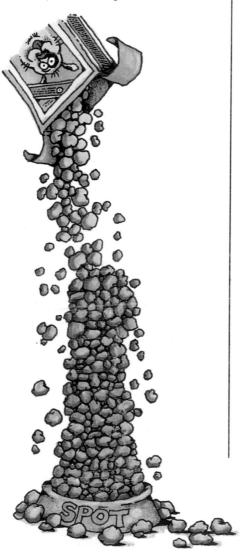

*Choosing a quality dog food from your pet shop is easy—deciding how much to feed may not be as straightforward. Feedings must always be carefully monitored.*

# Feeding Requirements

vegetables, egg yolk, cereal, cheese, brewer's yeast, and vitamin supplements. With all of the nutritionally complete commercial dog food products readily available, these time-consuming preparations really are unnecessary now. A great deal of money and research has resulted in foods that we can serve our dogs with confidence and pride; and most of these commercial foods have been developed along strict guidelines according to the size, weight, and age of your dog. These products are reasonably priced,

*Exercise and proper nutrition will go a long way toward keeping your Bedlington healthy and happy throughout his life.*

easy to find, and convenient to store.

## THE PUPPY'S MEALS

After a puppy has been fully weaned from its mother until approximately three months of age, it needs to be fed four times a day. In the morning and evening, offer kibble (dog meal) soaked in hot water or broth, to which you have added some canned meat-based food or fresh raw meat cut into small chunks. At noon and bedtime feed him a bit of kibble or whole-grain cereal moistened with milk (moistening, by the way, makes the food easier to digest, since dogs don't typically chew their food). From three to six months, increase the portion size and offer just three meals—one milk

*Keep a close eye on how much your pet eats each day. A change in appetite can be one of the first indications that something is wrong.*

and two meat. At six months, two meals are sufficient; at one year, a single meal can be given, supplemented with a few dry biscuits in the morning and evening. During the colder months, especially if your dog is active, you might want to mix in some wheat germ oil or corn oil or meat drippings with the meal to add extra calories. Remember to keep a bowl of cool, fresh water always on hand to help your dog regulate his body temperature and to aid in digestion.

From one year on, you may continue feeding the mature dog a single meal (in the evening, perhaps, when you have your supper), or you may prefer to divide this meal in two, offering half in the morning and the other half at night. Keep in mind that while puppies require foods in small chunks or nuggets, older dogs can handle larger pieces of food at mealtime. Discuss your dog's feeding schedule with your veterinarian; he can make suggestions about the right diet for your particular canine friend.

### COMPARISON SHOPPING
With so many fine dog-food products on the market today, there is something for

everyone's pet. You may want to serve dry food "as is" or mix it with warm water or broth. Perhaps you'll choose to combine dry food with fresh or canned preparations. Some canned foods contain all meat, but they are not complete; others are mixtures of meat and grains, which have been fortified with additional nutrients to make them more complete and balanced. There are also various packaged foods that can be served alone or as supplements and that can be left out for a few hours without spoiling. This self-feeding method, which works well for dogs that are not prone to weight problems, allows the animal to serve himself whenever he feels hungry. Many people who work during the day find these dry or semi-moist rations convenient to use, and these foods are great to bring along if you travel with your dog.

Be sure to read the labels carefully before you make your dog-food purchases. Most

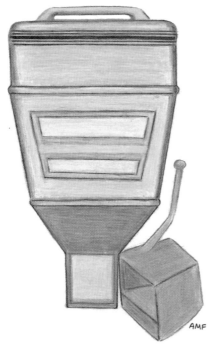

*Feeder bins are used by many kennel owners as well as pet owners. These devices help to conveniently store and distribute dry foods in a sanitary, efficient way.*

*Pet shops offer a variety of dry kibbles. Though the nutritional values of these foods are essentially equivalent, compare the manufacturer's labels.*

reputable pet-food manufacturers list the ingredients and the nutritional content right on the can or package. Instructions are usually included so that you will know how much to feed your dog to keep him thriving and in top condition. A varied, well-balanced diet that supplies the proper amounts of protein, carbohydrate, fat, vitamins, minerals, and water is important to keep your puppy healthy and to guarantee his normal development. Adjustments to the diet can be made, under your veterinarian's supervision, according to the individual puppy, his rate of growth, his activity level, and so on. Liquid or powder vitamin and mineral supplements, or those in tablet form, are available and can be given if you need to feel certain that the diet is balanced.

Proper coat, condition, and outlook on life are all dependent on good nutrition. Your Bedlington Terrier is certainly worth the effort.

## DEVELOPING GOOD EATING HABITS

Try to serve your puppy his meals at the same time each day and in the same location so that he will get used to his daily routine and develop good eating habits. A bit of raw egg, cottage cheese, or table scraps (leftover food from your own meals) can

*Feeding your dog is made easy by the use of sturdy non-tip, easy-clean bowls. Pet shops offer the best selection of colors, styles and sizes.*

be offered from time to time; but never accustom your dog to eating human "junk food." Cake, candy, chocolate, soda, and other snack foods are for people, not dogs. Besides, these foods provide only "empty" calories that your pet doesn't need if he is to stay healthy. Avoid offering spicy, fried, fatty, or starchy foods; rather, offer leftover meats, vegetables, and gravies. Get in the habit of feeding your puppy or your grown dog his *own* daily meals of dog food. If ever you are in doubt about what foods and how much to serve, consult your veterinarian.

# Feeding Requirements

## FEEDING GUIDELINES

Some things to bear in mind with regard to your dog's feeding regimen follow.

- Nutritional balance, provided by many commercial dog foods, is vital; avoid feeding a one-sided all-meat diet. Variety in the kinds of meat (beef, lamb, chicken, liver) or cereal grains (wheat, oats, corn) that

*Automatic feeders are handy modern devices, available from most good pet shops. Overfeeding can be a drawback of this method of feeding.*

you offer your dog is of secondary importance compared to the balance or "completeness" of dietary components.

- Always refrigerate opened canned food so that it doesn't spoil. Remember to remove all uneaten portions of canned or moistened food from the feeding dish as soon as the pup has finished his meal. Discard the leftover food immediately and thoroughly wash and dry the feeding dish, as a dirty dish is a breeding ground for harmful germs.

- When offering dry foods, always keep a supply of water on hand for your dog. Water should be made available at all times, even if dry foods are not left out for self-feeding. Each day the water dish should be washed with soap and hot water, rinsed well, and dried; a refill of clean, fresh water should be provided daily.

- Food and water should be served at room temperature, neither too hot nor too cold, so that it is more palatable for your puppy.

- Serve your pup's meals in sturdy hard-plastic, stainless steel, or earthenware containers, ones that won't tip over as the dog gulps his food down. Some bowls and dishes are weighted to prevent spillage, while others fit neatly into holders which offer

# THE WORLD'S LARGEST SELECTION OF PET AND ANIMAL BOOKS

T.F.H. Publications publishes more than 900 books covering many hobby aspects (dogs,

. . . BIRDS . .

. . CATS . . .

. . . ANIMALS . . .

. . . DOGS . .

. . FISH . . .

cats, birds, fish, small animals, etc.), plus books dealing with more purely scientific aspects of the animal world (such as books about fossils, corals, sea shells, whales and octopuses). Whether you are a beginner or an advanced hobbyist you will find exactly what you're looking for among our complete listing of books. For a free catalog fill out the form on the other side of this page and mail it today. All T.F.H. books are recyclable.

Since 1952, *Tropical Fish Hobbyist* has been the source of accurate, up-to-the-minute, and fascinating information on every facet of the aquarium hobby. Join the more than 50,000 devoted readers world-wide who wouldn't miss a single issue.

support. Feeding dishes should be large enough to hold each meal.

- Whenever the nutritional needs of your dog change—that is to say, when it grows older or if it becomes ill, obese, or pregnant; or if it starts to nurse its young—special diets are in order. Always contact your vet for advice on these special dietary requirements.

- Hard foods, such as biscuits and dog meal, should be offered regularly. Chewing on these hard, dry morsels helps the dog keep its teeth clean and its gums conditioned.

- Never overfeed your dog. If given the chance, he will accept and relish every in-between-meal tidbit you offer him. This pampering will only put extra weight on your pet and cause him to be unhealthy.

*New treats on the block by Chooz®. These crunchy dog bones are delectable and affordable.*

- Feed your puppy at the same regular intervals each day; reserve treats for special occasions or, perhaps, to reward good behavior.

- Do not encourage your dog to beg for food from the table while you are eating your meals.

- Food can be effectively used by the owner to train the dog. Doggie treats are practical and often nutritional—choose your chew treats choosily.

# FEEDING CHART

| Age and No. of Feedings Per Day | Weight in Lbs. | Weight in Kg. | Caloric Requirement kcal M.E./Day |
|---|---|---|---|
| **Puppies—Weaning to 3 months** Four per day | 1–3 3–6 6–12 12–20 15–30 | .5–1.4 1.4–2.7 2.7–5.4 5.4–9.1 6.8–13.6 | 124–334 334–574 574–943 943–1384 1113–1872 |
| **Puppies—3 to 6 months** Three per day | 3–10 5–15 12–25 20–40 30–70 | 1.4–4.5 2.3–6.8 5.4–11.3 9.1–18.2 13.6–31.8 | 334–816 494–1113 943–1645 1384–2352 1872–3542 |
| **Puppies—6 to 12 months** Two per day | 6–12 12–25 20–50 40–70 70–100 | 2.7–5.4 5.4–11.3 9.1–22.7 18.2–31.8 31.8–45.4 | 574–943 943–1645 1384–2750 2352–3542 3542–4640 |
| **Normally Active Adults** One or two per day | 6–12 12–25 25–50 50–90 90–175 | 2.7–5.4 5.4–11.3 11.3–22.7 22.7–40.8 40.8–79.4 | 286–472 472–823 823–1375 1375–2151 2151–3675 |

This chart presents general parameters of the dog's caloric requirements, based on weight. The total caloric intake comes from a complete, balanced diet of quality foods. To assist owners, dog food companies generally provide the nutritional information to their product right on the label.

# Accommodations

Puppies newly weaned from their mother and siblings should be kept warm at all times. As they get older, they can be acclimated gradually to cooler temperatures. When you purchase your dog, find out from the seller whether he is hardy and can withstand the rigors of outdoor living. Many breeds have been known to adapt well to a surprising number of environments, so long as they are given time to adjust. If your pup is to be an indoor for your pooch; or you may find that a heated garage or finished basement works well as your dog's living quarters. If your breed can tolerate living outside, you may want to buy or build him his own dog house with an attached run. It might be feasible to place his house in your fenced-in backyard. The breed that can live outdoors fares well when given access to some sort of warm, dry shelter during periods of inclement weather. As you begin thinking about where

companion, perhaps a dog bed in the corner of the family room will suffice; or you may want to invest in a crate for him to call his "home" whenever he needs to be confined for short intervals. You might plan to partition off a special room, or part of a room,

*A bed for your dog gives him a place to call his own. His bed should be placed in a warm, dry, draft-free area.*

your canine friend will spend most of his time, you'll want to consider his breed, his age, his temperament, his need for exercise, and the money, space, and resources you have available to house him.

your puppy something with which to snuggle, such as a laundered towel or blanket or an article of old clothing. Some dogs have been known to chew apart their beds and bedding, but you can easily channel this

### THE DOG BED

In preparing for your puppy's arrival, it is recommended that a dog bed be waiting for him so that he has a place to sleep and rest. If you have provided him with his own bed or basket, ensure that it is placed in a warm, dry, draft-free spot that is private but at the same time near the center of family activity. Refrain from placing his bed near the feed and water dishes or his toilet area. You may want to give

*Beds can have personality. Pet shops offer many different bedding options to the owner willing to explore.*

chewing energy into more constructive behavior simply by supplying him with some safe toys or a Nylabone® pacifier for gnawing. Pet shops stock dog beds, among other supplies that you might need for your pup. Select a bed that is roomy, comfortable, and easy to clean, keeping in mind that you may have to replace the smaller bed with a larger one as the puppy grows to adulthood. Remember to clean and disinfect the bed and sleeping area from time to time, as these can become parasitic playgrounds for fleas, lice, mites, and the like.

## THE CRATE

Although many dog lovers may cringe at the mere mention of the word *crate,* thinking of it as a cage or a cruel means of confinement, this handy piece of equipment can be put to good use for puppies and grown dogs alike. Even though you may love your dog to an extraordinary degree, you may not want him to have free reign of the house, particularly when you are not home to supervise him. If used properly, a crate can restrict your dog when it is not convenient to have him underfoot, *i.e.,* when guests are visiting or during your mealtimes.

A surprising number of dog owners, who originally had negative feelings about crating their dogs, have had great success using crates. The crate itself serves as a bed, provided it is furnished with bedding material, or it can be used as an indoor dog house. Not all dogs

*The wire crate is a most effective means to accelerate housebreaking and is the safest way to ensure that the puppy is safe when he cannot be supervised.*

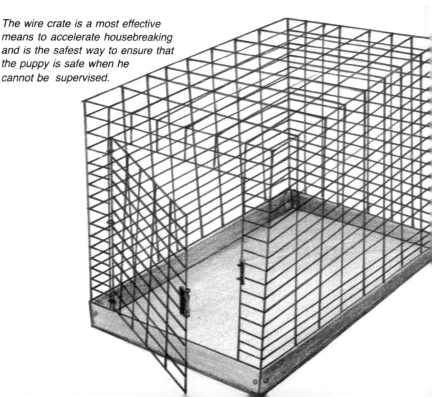

readily accept crates or being confined in them for short intervals, so for these dogs, another means of restriction must be found. But for those dogs that do adjust to spending time in these structures, the crate can be useful in many ways. The animal can be confined for a few hours while you are away from home or at work, or you can bring your

*If your living arrangement allows, an outdoor run connected to the house by a swinging pet door can provide an ideal accommodation for your dog.*

crated dog along with you in the car when you travel or go on vacation. Crates also prove handy as carriers whenever you have to transport a sick dog to the veterinarian.

Most crates are made of sturdy wire or plastic, and some of the collapsible models can be conveniently stored or folded so that they can be moved easily from room to room or from inside the house to the yard on a warm, sunny day. If you allow your puppy or grown dog to become acquainted with its crate by cleverly propping the door open and leaving some of his favorite toys inside, in no time he

will come to regard the crate as his own doggie haven. As with a dog bed, place the crate away from drafts in a dry, warm spot; refrain from placing food and water dishes in it, as these only crowd the space and offer opportunity for spillage.

If you need to confine your puppy so that he can't get into mischief while you're not home, remember to consider the animal's needs at all times. Select a large crate, one in which the dog can stand up and move around comfortably; in fact, bigger is better in this context. Never leave the animal confined for more than a few hours at a time without letting him out to exercise, play, and, if necessary, relieve himself. Never crate a dog for ten hours, for example, unless you keep the door to the crate open so that he can get out for food and water and to stretch a bit. If long intervals of confinement are necessary, consider placing the unlatched crate in a partitioned section of your house or apartment.

Crates have become the answer for many a dog owner faced with the dilemma of either getting rid of a destructive dog or living with him despite his bad habits. People who have neither the time nor the patience to train their dogs, or to modify undesirable behavior patterns, can at least restrain their pets during the times they can't be

*Traveling crates can provide safe and easy transport for your dog. Ventilation for travel is a most important consideration.*

there to supervise. So long as the crate is used in a humane fashion, whereby a dog is confined for no more than a few hours at any one time, it can figure importantly in a dog owner's life. Show dogs,

*The pet trade offers many commercially made dog houses and other outdoor living structures that make great temporary accommodations for your pet.*

incidentally, learn at an early age that much time will be spent in and out of crates while they are on the show circuit. Many canine celebrities are kept in their crates until they are called to ringside, and they spend many hours crated to and from the shows.

## THE DOG HOUSE

These structures, often made of wood, should be sturdy and offer enough room for your dog to stretch out in when it rests or sleeps. Dog houses that are elevated or situated on a platform protect the animal from cold and dampness that may seep through the ground. For the breeds that are temperature hardy and will live outdoors, a dog house is an excellent option for daytime occupancy. Owners who cannot provide indoor accommodations for their chosen dog should consider a smaller breed since no dog should lead an exclusively outdoor existence.

If you have no option but to accommodate your dog with only an outdoor house, it will be necessary to provide him with a more elaborate house, one that really protects him from the elements. Make sure the dog's house is constructed of waterproof materials. Furnish him with sufficient bedding to burrow into on a chilly night and provide extra insulation to keep

out drafts and wet weather. Add a partition (a kind of room divider which separates the entry area from the main sleeping space) inside his house or attach a swinging door to the entrance to help keep him warm when he is inside his residence. The

*Indoor-outdoor dog houses offer pest-free, sanitary conditions for your dog. These attractive living options can be acquired from pet shops, supply outlets or mail-order catalogues.*

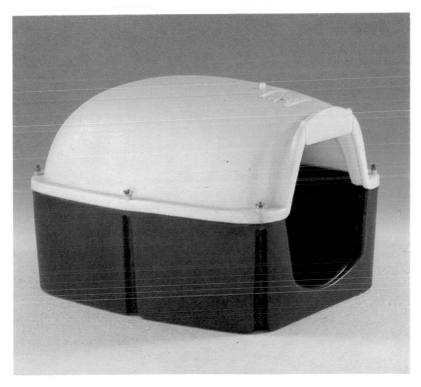

swinging door facilitates entry to and from the dog house, while at the same time it provides protection, particularly from wind and drafts.

Some fortunate owners whose yards are enclosed by high freedom is a dog kennel or run which attaches to or surrounds the dog's house. This restricts some forms of movement, such as running, perhaps, but it does provide ample room for walking, climbing, jumping, and

An anchored lead can provide efficient temporary restraint. This is not a viable substitute for a fenced-in yard and no dog should be left unsupervised on such a lead for any length of time.

fencing allow their dogs complete freedom within the boundaries of their property. In these situations, a dog can leave his dog house and get all the exercise he wants. Of course such a large space requires more effort to keep it clean. An alternative to complete backyard stretching. Another option is to fence off part of the yard and place the dog house in the enclosure. If you need to tether your dog to its house, make certain to use a fairly long lead so as not to hamper the animal's need to move and exercise his limbs.

## CLEANLINESS

No matter where your dog lives, either in or out of your home, be sure to keep him in surroundings that are as clean and sanitary as possible. His excrement should be removed and disposed of every day without fail. No dog should be forced to lie in his own feces. If your dog lives in his own house, the floor should be swept occasionally and the bedding should be changed regularly if it becomes soiled. Food and water dishes need to be scrubbed with hot water and detergent and rinsed well to remove all traces of soap. The water dish should be refilled with a supply of fresh water. The dog and his environment must be kept free of parasites (especially fleas and mosquitoes, which can carry disease) with products designed to keep these pests under control. Dog crates need frequent scrubbing, too, as do the floors of kennels and runs. Your pet must be kept clean and comfortable at all times; if you exercise strict sanitary control, you will keep disease and parasite infestation to a minimum.

## EXERCISE

A well-balanced diet and regular medical attention from a qualified veterinarian are essential in promoting good health for your dog, but so is

*Most cities and towns require dog owners to clean up after their pets. Commercial pooper scoopers can make curbing your dog more convenient and sanitary.*

daily exercise to keep him fit and mentally alert. Dogs that have been confined all day while their owners are at work or school need special attention. There should be some time set aside each day for play—a romp with a family member, perhaps. Not everyone is lucky enough to let his dog run through an open meadow or along a sandy beach, but even a ten-minute walk in the fresh air will do  Dogs that are house-bound, particularly those that live in apartments, need to

*Flying discs are popular with most dog owners, child and adult alike. Many dogs display a natural talent for Frisbee® games.*

be walked out-of-doors after each meal so that they can relieve themselves. Owners can make this daily ritual more pleasant both for themselves

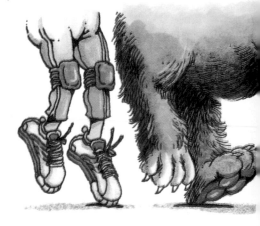

and their canine companions by combining the walk with a little "roughhousing," that is to say, a bit of fun and togetherness.

Whenever possible, take a stroll to an empty lot, a playground, or a nearby park. Attach a long lead to your dog's collar, and let him run and jump and tone his body through aerobic activity. This will help him burn calories and will keep him trim, and it will also help relieve tension and stress that may have had a chance to develop while you were away all day. For people who work Monday through Friday, weekend jaunts can be especially beneficial, since there will be more time to spend with your canine friend. You might want to engage him in a simple game of fetch with a stick or a rubber ball. Even such basic tricks as rolling over, standing on

by all means do it. Don't neglect your pet and leave him confined for long periods without attention from you or time for exercise.

the hindlegs, or jumping up (all of which can be done inside the home as well) can provide additional exercise. But if you plan to challenge your dog with a real workout to raise his heart rate, remember not to push him too hard without first warming up with a brisk walk. Don't forget to "cool him down" afterwards with a rhythmic trot until his heart rate returns to normal. Some dog owners jog with their dogs or take them along on bicycle excursions.

At the very least, however, play with your dog every day to keep him in good shape physically and mentally. If you can walk him outdoors, or better yet run with him in a more vigorous activity,

*Fitness and exercise are on the move. Getting in on the trim-and-active side ain't just a doggie obsession—owners should sneak in too!*

## EXERCISING FOR YOU AND YOUR DOG

Dogs are like people. They come in three weights: overweight, underweight, and the correct weight. It is fair to say that most dogs are in better shape than most humans who own them. The reason for this is that most dogs accept exercise without objection—people do not! Follow your dog's lead towards exercise and the complete enjoyment of the outdoors—your dog is the ideal work-out partner. There are toys

at your local pet shop which are designed just for that purpose: to allow you to play and exercise with your dog. Here are a few recommended exercise toys for you and your dog.

**Frisbee® Flying Discs** Most dog owners capitalize on the dog's natural instinct to fetch or retrieve, and the Frisbee® flying disc is standard fare for play. The original Frisbee® is composed of polyethylene plastic, ideal for flying and great for games of catch between two humans. Since humans don't usually chew on their flying discs, there is no need for a "chew-worthy" construction material. Dogs, on the other

*The most popular in flying discs designed especially for dogs is the Nylabone Frisbee®, a toy that outlasts plastic discs by ten times. The molded dog bone on the top makes for easy retrieves by your dog.*

hand, do chew on their Frisbees® and therefore should not be allowed to play with a standard original Frisbee®. These discs will be destroyed quickly by the dog and the rigid plastic can cause intestinal complications.

**Nylon Discs** More suitable for playing with dogs are the Frisbee® discs that are constructed from nylon. These durable Frisbee® discs are designed especially for dogs and the nearly indestructible manufacturing makes them ideal for aggressive chewing dogs. For play with dogs, the nylon discs called Nylabone Frisbee® are guaranteed to last ten times as long as the regular plastic Frisbee®. Owners should carefully consider the size of the nylon Frisbee® they purchase. A rule of thumb is choose the largest disc that your dog can comfortably carry. Nylabone manufactures two sizes only—toy and large—so the choice should be apparent.

**Polyurethane Flexible Floppy Flying Discs** The greatest advance in flying discs came with the manufacture of these discs from polyurethane. The polyurethane is so soft that it doesn't hurt you, your dog, or the window it might strike accidentally. The polyurethane Gumadisc® is floppy and soft. It can be folded and fits into your pocket. It is also much tougher than cheap plastics, and most pet shops guarantee that it will last ten times longer than cheap plastic discs.

Making the polyurethane discs even more suited to dog play is the fact that many of the Gumabone® Frisbee® Flexible Fly Discs have the advantage of a dog bone molded on the top. Very often a Frisbee® without the bone molded on the top is difficult for a dog to pick up

*Made of durable and flexible polyurethane, the Gumabone Frisbees® prove chew-worthy and good-smelling to dogs. These and other Nylabone® discs are available in pet shops and other stores.*

*Frisbee® is a trademark of the Kransco Company, California, and is used for their brand of flying disc.

when it lands on a flat surface. The molded ones enable the dog to grasp it with his mouth or turn it with his paw. Dogs love pawing at the bone and even chew on it occasionally.

This product has one further capacity—it doubles as a temporary drinking dish while out running, hiking and playing. The Gumabone Frisbee® flyers may also be flavored or scented, besides being annealed, so your dog can find it more easily if it should get lost in woods or tall grass.

with your canine friend. Basically, you play with the dog and the disc so the dog knows the disc belongs to him. Then you throw it continuously,

*Toys made for doggie tug-of-wars are popular with lots of pet owners. These tug toys are durable and last a long time.*

Flying discs manufactured by the Nylabone® Company may cost more than some of its imitators, but an owner can be assured that the product will last and not be quickly destroyed.

With most flying discs made for dogs comes an instruction booklet on how to use the disc

increasing the distance, so that the dog fetches it and brings it back to you.

The exercise for you comes in when your dog stops fetching it, or when you have a partner. The two of you play catch. You stand as far apart as available space allows—usually 30–35 m (100

*Great for the athletic dog and less-active owner are commercially designed retractable leads which give the dog much freedom when exercising in an open field or cleared area.*

feet) is more than enough room. You throw the disc to each other, arousing your dog's interest as he tries to catch it. When the disc is dropped or veers off, the dog grabs it and brings it back (hopefully). Obviously you will have to run to catch the disc before your dog does.

There are contests held all over the world where distance, height, and other characteristics are measured competitively. Ask your local pet shop to help you locate a Frisbee® Club near you.

**Tug Toys** A tug toy is a hard rubber, cheap plastic, or polyurethane toy which allows a

*Frisbee® is a trademark of the Kransco Company, California, and is used for their brand of flying disc.

*The more consideration given to the canine's needs, the better the outdoor accommodations will be. Owners planning an outdoor kennel set-up must consider the elements (sun, rain, and wind) as well as sanitation and security.*

dog and his owner to have a game of tug-o-war. The owner grips one end while the dog grips the other—then they pull. The polyurethane flexible tug toy is the best on the market at the present time. Your pet shop will have one to show you. The polyurethane toys are clear in color and stay soft forever. Cheap plastic tug toys are indisputably dangerous, and the hard-rubber tug toys get brittle too fast and are too stiff for most dogs; however, there *is* a difference in price—just ask the advice of any pet shop operator.

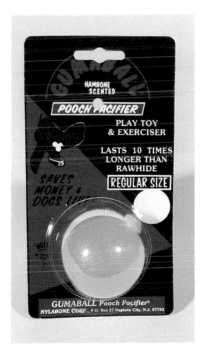

**Balls** Nobody has to tell you about playing ball with your dog. The reminder you may need is that you should not throw the ball where traffic might interfere with the dog's catching or fetching of it. The ball should not be cheap plastic (a dog's worst enemy as far as toys are concerned) but made of a substantial material. Balls made of nylon are practically indestructible, but they are very hard and must be rolled, never thrown. The same balls made of polyurethane are great—they bounce and are soft. The Nylaballs® and Gumaballs® are scented and flavored, and dogs can easily find them when lost.

Other manufacturers make balls of almost every substance, including plastic, cotton, and wood. Soft balls, baseballs, tennis balls, and so on, have all been used by dog owners who want their dogs to play with them in a game of catch. A strong caveat is that you use only those balls made especially for dogs.

*It pays to invest in entertainment toys and exercise devices which are marketed particularly for dogs. These products outlast everyday play things and are much safer for your pet. The Gumaball® is a great example of a dog toy worth the price of admission.*

Housebreaking is required training for all puppies and even some older dogs who come in to new homes. There are many experience-based rules for the housebreaking owner to follow, including the use of a restricted area and close supervision. If approached thoughtfully and intelligently, housebreaking should proceed smoothly to its completion.

# Housebreaking and Training

The value of the news may be waning in recent years, but newspaper will always have a worthwhile purpose to the new dog owner.

## HOUSEBREAKING

The new addition to your family may already have received some basic house training before his arrival in your home. If he has not, remember that a puppy will want to relieve himself about half a dozen times a day; it is up to you to specify where and when he should "do his business." Housebreaking is your first training concern and should begin the moment you bring the puppy home.

Ideally, puppies should be taken outdoors after meals, as a full stomach will exert pressure on the bladder and colon. What

goes into the dog must eventually come out; the period after his meal is the most natural and appropriate time. When he eliminates, he should be praised, for this will increase the likelihood of the same thing happening after every meal. He should also be encouraged to

that your pet will associate the act of elimination with a particular word of your choice rather than with a particular time or place which might not always be convenient or available. So whether you are visiting an unfamiliar place or don't want to go outside with your dog in sub-

*Housebreaking pads, used by many cautious owners instead of the ever trusty press, can be purchased in pet shops and pet supply outlets.*

use the same area and will probably be attracted to it after frequent use.

Some veterinarians maintain that a puppy can learn to urinate and defecate on command, if properly trained. The advantage of this conditioning technique is

zero temperatures, he will still be able to relieve himself when he hears the specific command word. Elimination will occur after this "trigger" phrase or word sets up a conditioned reflex in the dog, who will eliminate anything contained in his bladder or bowel upon hearing it. The shorter the word, the more you can repeat it and imprint it on your dog's memory.

Your chosen command word should be given simultaneously with the sphincter opening events in order to achieve perfect and rapid conditioning. This is why it is important to familiarize yourself with the tell-tale signs preceding your puppy's elimination process. Then you will be prepared to say the word at the crucial moment. There is usually a sense of urgency on the dog's part; he will soon learn to associate the act with the word. One word of advice, however, if you plan to try out this method: never use the puppy's name or any other word which he might frequently hear about the house—you can imagine the result!

Finally, remember that any training takes time. Such a conditioned response can be obtained with intensive practice with any normal, healthy dog over six weeks of age. Even Pavlov's salivating dogs required fifty repetitions before the desired response was achieved.

*Crates assist in potty-training the puppy. The dog's natural instinct is never to soil his sleeping area.*

may follow a sniffing and circling pattern which you will soon recognize. It is important to use the command in his usual area only when you know the puppy can eliminate, i.e., when his stomach or bladder is full. He

Patience and persistence will eventually produce results—do not lose heart!

Indoors, sheets of newspapers can be used to cover the specific area where your dog should relieve himself. These should be placed some distance away from his sleeping and feeding area, as a puppy will not urinate or defecate where he eats. When the newspapers are changed, the bottom papers should be placed on top of the new ones in order to reinforce the purpose of

the run of the house, the sheer size of the place will seem overwhelming and confusing and he might leave his "signature" on your furniture or clothes! There will be time later to familiarize him gradually with his new surroundings.

*The choke collar and walking lead are commonly used in training.*

the papers by scent as well as by sight. The puppy should be praised during or immediately after he has made use of this particular part of the room. Each positive reinforcement increases the possibility of his using that area again.

When he arrives, it is advisable to limit the puppy to one room, usually the kitchen, as it most likely has a linoleum or easily washable floor surface. Given

## PATIENCE, PERSISTENCE, AND PRAISE

As with a human baby, you must be patient, tolerant, and understanding of your pet's mistakes, making him feel loved and wanted, not rejected and isolated. You wouldn't hit a baby for soiling his diapers, as you would realize that he was not yet able to control his bowel movements; be as compassionate with your canine infant. Never rub his nose in his excreta. Never indulge in the common practice of punishing him with a rolled-up newspaper. Never hit a puppy with your hand. He will only become "hand-shy" and learn to fear you. Usually the punishment is meted out sometime after the offense and loses its efficacy, as the bewildered dog cannot connect the two events. Moreover, by association, he will soon learn to be afraid of you and anything to do with newspapers—including, perhaps, that area where he is *supposed* to relieve himself!

*A simple dog collar or leash can be deceiving. Never be afraid to ask your pet shop proprietor exactly how a particular device is intended to work.*

Most puppies are eager to please. Praise, encouragement, and reward (particularly the food variety) will produce far better results than any scolding or physical punishment. Moreover, it is far better to dissuade your puppy from doing certain things, such as chewing on chair legs or other furniture, by making those objects particularly distasteful to him. Some pet shops stock bitter apple sprays or citronella compounds for application to furniture legs. These products are generally safer than old-fashioned home remedies. An owner may soon discover that application of these products may indeed make it seem as if the object itself was administering the punishment whenever he attempted to chew it. He probably wouldn't need a second reminder and your furniture will remain undamaged.

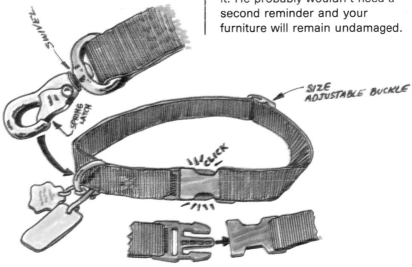

Remember that the reason a dog has housebreaking or behavior problems is because his owner has allowed them to develop. This is why you must begin as you intend to continue, letting your dog know what is acceptable and unacceptable behavior. It is also important that you be consistent in your

*A choke collar can be an effective training tool when properly used.*

demands; you cannot feed him from the dining room table one day and then punish him when he begs for food from your dinner guests.

## TRAINING

You will want the newest member of your family to be welcomed by everyone; this will

not happen if he urinates in every room of the house or barks all night! He needs training in the correct forms of behavior in this new human world. You cannot expect your puppy to become the perfect pet overnight. He needs your help in his socialization process. Training greatly facilitates and enhances the relationship of the dog to his owner and to the rest of society. A successfully trained dog can be taken anywhere and behave well with anyone. Indeed, it is that one crucial word—*training*—which can transform an aggressive animal into a peaceful, well-behaved pet. Now, how does this "transformation" take place?

## WHEN AND HOW TO TRAIN

Like housebreaking, training should begin as soon as the puppy enters the house. The formal training sessions should be short but frequent, for example, ten to fifteen minute periods three times a day. These are much more effective than long, tiring sessions of half an hour which might soon become boring. You are building your relationship with your puppy during these times, so make them as enjoyable as possible. It is a good idea to have these sessions *before* the puppy's meal, not after it when he wouldn't feel like exerting himself; the dog will then

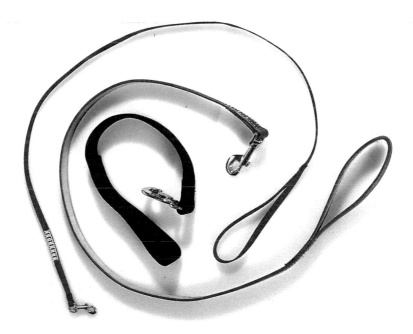

associate something pleasurable with his training sessions and look forward to them.

## THE COLLAR AND LEASH

Your puppy should become used to a collar and leash as soon as possible. If he is very young, a thin, choke-chain collar can be used, but you will need a larger and heavier one for training when he is a little older. Remember to have his name and address on an identification tag attached to his collar, as you don't want to lose your pet if he should happen to leave your premises and explore the neighborhood!

*Nylon and leather leads are the most popular with pet owners.*

Let the puppy wear his collar until he is used to how it feels. After a short time he will soon become accustomed to it and you can attach the leash. He might resist your attempts to lead him or simply sit down and refuse to budge. Fight him for a few minutes, tugging on the leash if necessary, then let him relax for the day. He won't be trained until he learns that he must obey the pull under any circumstance, but this will take a few sessions. Remember that a dog's period of concentration is short, so LITTLE and OFTEN is the wisest course of action—and patience is the password to success.

*For safety purposes, as well as the comfort of your pet, be sure to choose the right-sized collar and a sensible leash for your daily walks.*

## GIVING COMMANDS

When you begin giving your puppy simple commands, make them as short as possible and use the same word with the same meaning at all times, for example, "Heel," "Sit," and "Stay." You must be consistent; otherwise your puppy will become confused. The dog's name should prefix all commands to attract his attention. Do not become impatient with him however many times you have to repeat your command.

A good way to introduce the "Come" command is by calling the puppy when his meal is ready. Once this is learned, you can call your pet to you at will, always remembering to praise him for his prompt obedience. This "reward," or positive reinforcement, is such a crucial part of training that a Director of the New York Academy of Dog Training constructed his whole teaching program upon the methods of "Love, Praise, and Reward." Incidentally, if you use the command "Come," use it every time. Don't switch to "Come here" or "Come boy," as this will only confuse your dog.

It is worth underlining the fact that punishment is an ineffective teaching technique. We have already seen this in housebreaking. For example, if your pup should run away, it would be senseless to beat him when he eventually returns; he would only connect the punishment with his return, not with running away! In addition, it is unwise to call him to you to punish him, as he will soon learn not to respond when you call his name.

*Harnesses can be used for daily walks, though some dogs do not find them comfortable. Heavily coated dogs especially may object, and the harness can eventually wear on the dog's coat.*

## SOME SPECIFIC COMMANDS

**"Sit"** This is one of the easiest and most useful commands for your dog to learn, so it is a good idea to begin with it. The only equipment required is a leash, a collar, and a few tasty tidbits. Take your dog out for some exercise before his meal. After about five minutes, call him to you, praise him when he arrives,

*Praise must be given when the dog correctly assumes the sit position. If praise is given before sitting or after the dog makes motion to rise, the dog may become confused.*

and slip his collar on him. Hold the leash tightly in your right hand; this should force the dog's head up and focus his attention on you. As you say "Sit" in a loud, clear voice, with your left hand press steadily on his rump until he is in a sitting position. As soon as he is in the correct position, praise him and give him the tidbit you have in your hand. Now wait a few minutes to let him rest and repeat the routine. Through repetition, the dog soon associates the word with the act. Never make the lesson too long. Eventually your praise will be reward enough for your puppy. Other methods to teach this command exist, but this one, executed with care and moderation, has proven the most effective.

**"Sit-Stay/Stay"** To teach your pet to remain in one place or "stay" on your command, first of all order him to the sitting position at your side. Lower your left hand with the flat of your palm in front of his nose and your fingers pointing downwards. Hold the leash high and taut behind his head so that he cannot move. Speak the command "Sit-stay" and, as you are giving it, step in front of him. Repeat the command and tighten the leash so the animal cannot follow you. Walk completely around him, repeating the command and keeping him notionless by holding the leash at arm's length above him to check his movement. When he remains in this position for about fifteen seconds, you can begin the second part of the training. You will have to exchange the leash for a nylon cord or rope about twenty to thirty feet long. Repeat the whole routine from the beginning and be ready to prevent any movement towards you with a sharp "Sit-stay." Move around him in ever-widening circles until you are about fifteen feet away from him. If he still remains seated, you can pat yourself on the back! One useful thing to remember is that the dog makes associations with what you say, how you say it, and what you do while you are saying it. Give this command in a firm, clear tone of voice, perhaps using an admonishing forefinger raised, warning the dog to "stay."

*Timing is all-important in sit training—be sure to say "sit" and press down on the dog's rump at the same time.*

**"Heel"** When you walk your dog, you should hold the leash firmly in your right hand. The dog should walk on your left so you have the leash crossing your body. This enables you to have greater control over the dog.

Let your dog lead you for the first few moments so that he fully understands that freedom can be his if he goes about it properly. He already knows that when he wants to go outdoors the leash and collar are

necessary, so he has respect for the leash. Now, if he starts to pull in one direction while walking, all you do is *stop walking.* He will walk a few steps and then find that he can't walk any further. He will then turn and look into your face. *This is the crucial point!* Just stand there for a moment and stare right back at him . . . now walk another ten feet and stop again. Again your dog will probably walk to the end of the leash, find he can't go any further, and turn around and look again. If he starts to pull and jerk, just stand there. After he quiets down, bend down and comfort him, as he may be frightened. Keep up this training until he learns not to outwalk you.

Once the puppy obeys the pull of the leash, half of your training is accomplished. "Heeling" is a necessity for a well-behaved dog, so teach him to walk beside you, head even with your knee. Nothing looks sadder than a big dog taking his helpless owner for a walk. It is annoying to passers-by and other dog owners to have a large dog, however friendly, bear down on them and entangle dogs, people, and packages.

To teach your dog, start off walking briskly, saying "Heel" in a firm voice. Pull back with a sharp jerk if he lunges ahead, and if he lags repeat the command and tug on the leash, not allowing him to drag behind. After the dog has learned to heel at various speeds on leash, you can remove it and practice heeling free, but have it ready to snap on again as soon as he wanders.

*When in the heel position, the dog should be at your left side. The lead should be held in your right hand, loosely except when checking him back to the desired position.*

**"Come"** Your dog has already learned to come to you when you call his name. Why? Because you only call him when his food is ready or when you wish to play with him or praise him. Outdoors such a response is more difficult to achieve, if he is happily playing by himself or with other dogs, so he must be trained to come to you when he is called. To teach him to come, let him reach the end of a long lead, then give the command, gently pulling him towards you at the same time. As soon as he associates the word *come* with the action of moving towards you, pull only when he does not respond immediately. As he starts to come, move back to make him learn that he must come from a distance as well as when he is close to you. Soon you may be able to practice without a leash, but if he is slow to come or actively disobedient, go to him and pull him toward you, repeating the command. Always remember to reward his successful completion of a task.

**"Down"** Teaching the "down" command ideally begins while your dog is still a pup. During

*Be gentle and reassuring with your dog, especially during the early stages of the down training—he may not understand what you are doing and may even feel threatened.*

*Correct behavior deserves positive reinforcement. When your dog heels, let him know how pleased you are by giving a kind word or reward.*

puppyhood your dog frequently will lie down, as this position is one of the dog's most natural positions. Invest some time, and keep close watch over your pup. Each time he begins to lie, repeat in a low convincing tone the word "down." If for the first day of training, you concur a majority of the dog's sitting with your commands and continue with reinforcement and moderate praise your pup should conquer the "down" command in no time.

Teaching the "down" command to a mature dog likely will require more effort. Although the lying position is still natural to a dog, his being forced into it is not. Some dogs may react with

*Once he is in the correct down position, lavish praise will tell him that he is doing well.*

fear, anger, or confusion. Others may accept the process and prove quick learners. Have your dog sit and face you. If he is responsive and congenial, gently take his paws, and slowly pull them towards you; give the "down" command as he approaches the proper position. Repeat several times: moderate reinforcement of this procedure should prove successful.

For the dog that responds with anger or aggression, attach a lead (and a muzzle) and have the dog sit facing you at a close distance. There should be a J-loop formed by the lead. With moderate force, relative to the size and strength of your dog, step on the J-loop, forcing the dog down, while repeating the command "down" in a low forceful tone. When the dog is down, moderate praise should be given. If the dog proves responsive, you may attempt extending his legs to the "down" position—leaving the muzzle on, of course. Daily reinforcement of the training method will soon yield the desired results. The keys to remember are: patience, persistence, and praise.

# Behavior Modification

"Problems with the Barking Dog" and "Aggressive Behavior and Dominance" are extracts from the veterinary monograph *Canine Behavior* (a compilation of columns from *Canine Practice,* a journal published by Veterinary Practice Publishing Company).

## PROBLEMS WITH THE BARKING DOG

One of the most frequent complaints about canine behavior is barking. Aside from the biting dog, the barking dog is probably the pet peeve of many non-dog owners. I know of at least one city in which owners of dogs that bark excessively, and for which there are complaints on file, are required to take steps to eliminate the barking.

Canine practitioners are drawn into problems with barking when they are asked for their advice in helping an owner come up with a solution or, as a last resort, when they are requested to perform a debarking operation or even euthanasia. In this column I will deal with some of the factors that apparently cause dogs to bark and suggest some corrective approaches.

Barking is, of course, a natural response for many dogs. They have an inherited predisposition to bark as an alarm when other dogs or people approach their territory. Alarm barking makes

*Only in the most extreme situations may trainers recommend electric-shock collars for correcting a dog's misbehavior.*

many dogs valuable as household watchdogs and is not necessarily undesirable behavior. With a different vocal tone and pattern, dogs bark when they are playing with each other. On occasion dogs have a tendency to bark back at other dogs or join in with other barking dogs.

In addition to inherited barking tendencies, dogs can also learn to bark if the barking is followed, at least sometimes, by a reward. Thus dogs may bark when they wish to come in the house or to get out of a kennel. Some dogs are trained to bark upon hearing the command "speak" for a food reward.

One of the first approaches to take when discussing a barking problem is to determine if the behavior is a manifestation of a natural (inherited) tendency or is learned behavior which has been rewarded in the past.

praise again when it barks after being told to "speak," it will eventually stop this type of barking. This is the process of extinction and it implies that the behavior must be repeated but never again rewarded.

A more practical example of the possible use of extinction

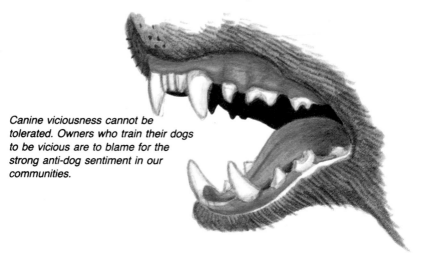

*Canine viciousness cannot be tolerated. Owners who train their dogs to be vicious are to blame for the strong anti-dog sentiment in our communities.*

## Can Barking Be Extinguished?

Extinction, as a way of eliminating a behavioral problem, may be considered when it is clear that the behavior has been learned and when one can identify the specific rewarding or reinforcing factors that maintain the behavior.

For example, the dog that barks upon hearing the command "speak" is periodically rewarded with food and praise. If a dog is never, ever given food or

would be in dealing with the dog that apparently barks because, at least occasionally, it is allowed in the house. By not allowing the dog in the house until the barking has become very frequent and loud, the owners may have shaped the barking behavior to that which is the most objectionable. If the dog is never allowed in the house again when barking, the barking should eventually be extinguished—at least theoretically.

## How Should Punishment Be Used?

Sometimes it is not feasible to attempt to extinguish barking even if it seems to be the case that the behavior was learned. This brings up the advisability of punishment. Clients who seek advice in dealing with a barking problem may already have employed some type of punishment such as shouting at the dog or throwing something at it. That this type of punishment is ineffective is attested to by the fact that the client is seeking advice. By shouting at a dog or hitting, a person interferes with what effect the punishment may have on the behavior itself through the arousal of autonomic reactions and escape attempts or submissive responses by the dog.

## The Water Bucket Approach

I am rather impressed by the ingenuity of some dog owners in

*Sound-wave bark-control collars emit a noise that is inaudible to man but discomforting to the canine. These should not be used without professional supervision.*

coming up with ways to punish a dog for barking without being directly involved in administering the punishment. One such harried dog owner I talked to, who was also a veterinarian, was plagued by his dog's barking in the kennel commencing at about 1:30 a.m. every night. A platform to hold a bucket of water was constructed over the area of the kennel in which the dog usually chose to bark. Through a system of hinges, ropes, and pulleys, a mechanism was devised so that the dog owner could pull a rope from his bedroom window, dumping a bucket of water on the dog when he started to bark. The bucket was suspended such that once it was dumped, it

*Muzzles may prevent biting, but the root cause of biting must be extracted if the dog is to live as a trusted member of the human family.*

uprighted itself and the owner could fill it again remotely by turning on a garden hose. After two appropriate dunkings, the dog's barking behavior was apparently eliminated.

In advising a client on the type of punishment discussed above, keep in mind one important consideration. From the time the owner is ready to administer punishment for barking, every attempt should be made to punish all undesirable barking from that point on and not to allow excessively long periods of barking to go unpunished. Thus it may be necessary to keep a dog indoors when away unless the dog will be punished for barking when the owner is gone.

**Alternative Responses** Barking dogs are, and probably always will be, one of the enduring problems of dog owners. Barking is relatively effortless, and it is such a natural response for many dogs that it is admittedly hard to eliminate with either punishment or a program of conditioning non-barking. In some instances it may be advisable to forget about eliminating barking and to suggest that the problem be dealt with by changing the circumstances which lead to barking. For example, a dog that

*Pet gates are used to confine a dog to certain areas of the house. The dog must learn to accept any such restrictions and not attempt to overcome them.*

barks continuously in the backyard while the owners are away may not bark if left in the house while they are gone. But the problem of keeping the dog in the house may be related to inadequate house training or the dog's shedding hair or climbing onto the furniture. It may be easier to correct these latter behavioral problems than it is to change the barking behavior.

## AGGRESSIVE BEHAVIOR AND DOMINANCE

Aggressiveness can have many causes. Determining what kind of aggression an animal is manifesting is a prerequisite to successful treatment of the behavior. A frequent problem that is presented to the practitioner is one of aggression related to dominance.

Dogs, which are social animals, have a hierarchal system of dominance within their pack. This predisposition to take a dominant or submissive position relative to fellow canines also occurs in relationship to people. Only in unusual situations would a submissive dog threaten a dominant animal, and almost never would it physically assault its superior. The dominant dog, however, frequently threatens submissive individuals to maintain its position. In a household setting, a person may be the object of threats, and when the person backs off, the dog's position is reassured. The aggressive behavior is also reinforced, and when behavior is reinforced it is likely to recur.

**Case History** The following is a typical case history of a dog presented for aggression stemming from dominance.

Max was a two-year-old intact male Cocker Spaniel. He had been acquired by Mr. Smith, one year prior to his owner's marriage, as a puppy. He liked and was well liked by both Mr. and Mrs. Smith. He frequently solicited and received attention from both people. However, several times over the last few months, Max had snapped at Mrs. Smith and repeatedly growled at her. A detailed anamnesis revealed that such incidents usually occurred in situations where the dog wanted his own way or did not want to be bothered. He would growl if asked to move off a chair or if persistently commanded to do a specific task. He growled if Mrs. Smith came between him and a young female Cocker Spaniel acquired a year ago. He also refused to let Mrs. Smith take anything from his possession. Max never showed any of these aggressive behaviors toward Mr. Smith or strangers. Admittedly he did not have much opportunity to demonstrate such behaviors toward strangers. A description of the dog's body and facial postures and circumstances under which the aggression occurred did not indicate that this was a case of fear-induced aggression, but rather one of assertion of dominance.

Mrs. Smith's reaction to the aggression was always to retreat, and, hence, the dog was rewarded for his assertiveness. She had never physically disciplined the dog and was afraid to do so. To encourage her to physically take control of the dog would likely have resulted in her being bitten. The dominance-submissive relationship had to be reversed in a more subtle manner.

**Instructions to Client** Mrs. Smith was instructed to avoid all situations which might evoke any aggressive signs from Max. This was to prevent any further reinforcement of his growling and threats.

Both she and her husband were not to indiscriminately pet or show affection towards the dog. For the time being, if Max solicited attention from Mr. Smith, he was to ignore the dog. Mrs. Smith was to take advantage of Max's desire for attention by giving him a command which he had to obey before she praised and petted him. She was also to take advantage of high motivation levels for other activities whenever such situations arose. Max had to obey a command before she gave him anything—before she petted him, before she let him out or in, etc.

Mrs. Smith also was to assume total care of the dog and coveted food rewards as well as praise. These were entirely fun and play sessions—but within a few days the dog had acquired the habit of quickly responding to commands. And this habit transferred over to the non-game situations.

*There is a wide variety of collars and harnesses available to the dog owner. Talk with your pet shop proprietor to determine which one best satisfies your needs.*

become "the source of all good things in life" for Max. She was to feed him, take him on walks, play with him, etc.

Mrs. Smith also spent 5–10 minutes a day teaching Max simple parlor tricks and obedience responses for

**Results** Within a few weeks, Max had ceased to growl and threaten Mrs. Smith in situations that he previously had. He would move out of her way or lie quietly when she would pass by him. She could order him off the furniture and handle the female

# Behavior Modification

Cocker Spaniel without eliciting threats from Max.

Mrs. Smith still felt that she would not be able to take the objects from Max's possession. Additional instructions were given to her. She then began placing a series of objects at progressively closer distances to the dog while the dog was in a sit-stay position. After she placed the object on the floor for a short time, she would pick it up. If the dog was still in a sit-stay (which it always was), he received a reward of cheese and verbal praise. Eventually the objects were to be placed and removed from directly in front of the dog. At first she was to use objects that the dog did not care much about and then progressively use more coveted items. This was what she was

*Treats can be effective in shaping behavior and establishing a rapport with your pet.*

supposed to do, but before she actually had completed the program she called in excitedly to report that she had taken a piece of stolen food and a household ornament from Max's mouth. And he didn't even object! She said she had calmly told Max to sit. He did. He was so used to doing so, in the game and other situations, that the response was now automatic. She walked over, removed the item from his mouth, and praised him.

Mrs. Smith did resume the systematic presentation of objects and put the dog on an intermittent schedule of food and praise reinforcement during the practice sessions. Mr. Smith again began interacting with Max.

A progress check six months later indicated Max was still an obedient dog and had definitely assumed a submissive position relative to both of his owners. The dominance hierarchy between Max and Mrs. Smith had been reversed *without resorting to any physical punishment.* Mrs. Smith was instructed to reinforce her dominance position by frequently giving Max a command and reinforcing him for the appropriate response.

**Summary** The essential elements in treatment of such cases are as follows. First, of course, there must be a correct

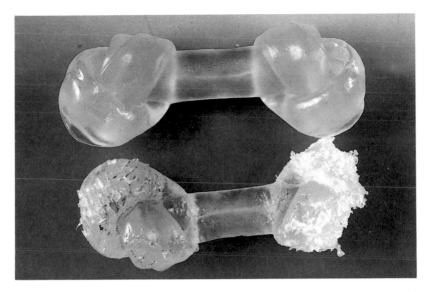

*Owners must take an active part in shaping their dog's behavior. Providing a sensible chew device can help alleviate an animal's frustration and thereby eliminate some undesirable behavior.*

diagnosis of what kind of aggressive behavior is occurring. During the course of treatment, the submissive person(s) should avoid all situations that might evoke an aggressive attitude by the dog. All other family members should totally ignore the dog during the treatment interim. The person most dominated by the dog should take over complete care of the dog in addition to spending 5–10 minutes a day teaching the dog tricks or simple obedience commands (sit-stay is a useful one to gain control of the dog in subsequent circumstances). These should be fun-and-games situations. Food rewards are highly recommended in addition to simple praise.

The person submissive to the dog should take the opportunity to give the dog a command, which must be obeyed, before doing anything pleasant for the dog.

It must be emphasized to the owner that no guarantee can be made that the dog will never threaten or be aggressive again. What is being done, as with all other aggression cases, is an attempt to reduce the likelihood, incidence, and intensity of occurrence of the aggressive behavior.

## DESTRUCTIVE TENDENCIES

It is ironical but true that a dog's destructive behavior in the home may be proof of his love for his owner. He may be trying to get more attention from his owner or, in other cases, may be expressing his frustration at his owner's absence. An abundance of unused energy may also contribute to a dog's destructive behavior, and therefore the owner should ensure that his dog has, at least, twenty minutes of vigorous exercise a day.

As a dog's destructive tendencies may stem from his desire to get more attention from his owner, the latter should devote specific periods each day to his dog when he is actively interacting with him. Such a period should contain practice obedience techniques during which the owner can reward the dog with his favorite food as well as praise and affection.

Planned departure conditioning is one specific technique which has been used to solve the problem of destructive tendencies in a puppy. It eventually ensures the dog's good behavior during the owner's absence. A series of short departures, which are identical to real departures, should condition the dog to behave well in the owner's absence. How is this to be achieved? Initially, the departures are so short (2–5 minutes) that the dog has no opportunity to be destructive. The dog is always rewarded for having been good when the owner returns. Gradually the duration of the departures is increased. The departure time is also varied so that the dog does not know when the owner is going to return. Since a different kind of behavior is now expected, it is best if a new stimulus or "atmosphere" is introduced into the training sessions to permit the dog to distinguish these departures as different from previous departures when he was destructive.

This new stimulus could be the sound of the radio or television. The association which the dog will develop is that whenever the "signal" or "stimulus" is on, the owner will return in an unknown period of time and, if the dog has not been destructive, he will be rewarded. As with the daily owner-dog interaction, the food reward is especially useful.

If the dog misbehaves during his owner's absence, the owner should speak sternly to him and isolate him from social contact for at least thirty minutes. (Puppies hate to be ignored.) Then the owner should conduct another departure of a shorter time and generously reward good behavior when he returns. The owner should progress slowly enough in the program so that once the departure has been initiated, the dog is never given an opportunity to make a mistake.

If planned departures are working satisfactorily, the departure time may gradually be extended to several hours. To reduce the dog's anxiety when left alone, he should be given a "safety valve" such as the indestructible Nylabone® to play with and chew on.

*While crates may be used principally for sleeping and traveling, some owners might opt to employ a crate for disciplining a dog, rather like sending a naughty child to his room.*

# Health Care

From the moment you purchase your puppy, the most important person in both your lives becomes your veterinarian. His

Bandaging a minor cut on the paw pad is one of many basic first-aid techniques that the dog owner should learn.

professional advice and treatment will ensure the good health of your pet. The vet is the first person to call when illness or accidents occur. Do *not* try to be your own veterinarian or apply human remedies to canine diseases. However, just as you would keep a first aid kit handy for minor injuries sustained by members of your family at home, so you should keep a similar kit prepared for your pet.

First aid for your dog would consist of stopping any bleeding, cleaning the wound, and preventing infection. Thus your kit might contain medicated powder, gauze bandages, and adhesive tape to be used in case of cuts. If the cut is deep and bleeding profusely, the bandage should be applied very tightly to help in the formation of a clot. A tight bandage should not be kept in place longer than necessary, so take your pet to the veterinarian immediately.

Walking or running on a cut pad prevents the cut from

*Thoroughly clean the injury with peroxide and apply an antibiotic. Then place the injured pad in sterile gauze, secure with first-aid tape, and replace daily.*

healing. Proper suturing of the cut and regular changing of the bandages should have your pet's wound healed in a week to ten days. A minor cut should be covered with a light bandage, for you want as much air as possible to reach the wound. Do not apply wads of cotton to a wound, as they will stick to the area and may cause contamination.

You should also keep some hydrogen peroxide available, as it is useful in cleaning wounds and is also one of the best and simplest emetics known. Cotton applicator swabs are useful for applying ointment or removing debris from the eyes. A pair of tweezers should also be kept handy for removing foreign bodies from the dog's neck, head or body.

Nearly everything a dog might contract in the way of sickness has basically the same set of symptoms: loss of appetite, diarrhea, dull eyes, dull coat, warm and/or runny nose, and a high temperature. Therefore, it is most important to take his temperature at the first sign of illness. To do this, you will need a rectal thermometer which should be lubricated with petroleum jelly. Carefully insert it into the rectum, holding it in place for at least two minutes. It must be held firmly; otherwise there is the danger of its being sucked up into the rectum or slipping out, thus giving an

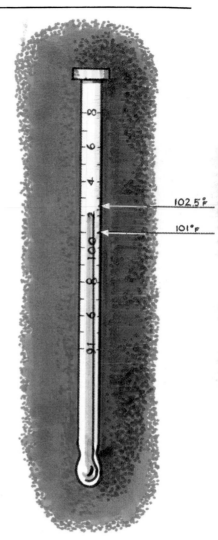

The normal temperature for the average dog ranges from 101°F to 102.5°F. This may vary during sleeping and exercise time.

113

inaccurate reading. The normal temperature for a dog is between 101° and 102.5°F. If your pet is seriously ill or injured in an accident, your veterinarian will advise you what to do before he arrives.

## SWALLOWING FOREIGN OBJECTS

Most of us have had experience with a child swallowing a foreign object. Usually it is a small coin; occasionally it may be a fruit pit or something more dangerous. Dogs, *as a general rule,* will not swallow anything which isn't edible. There are, however, many dogs that swallow pebbles or small shiny objects such as pins, coins, and bits of cloth and plastic. This is especially true of dogs that are offered so-called "chew toys."

Chew toys are available in many sizes, shapes, colors and materials. Some even have whistles which sound when the dog's owner plays with it or when the dog chomps on it quickly. Most dogs attack the whistle first, doing everything possible to make it stop squeaking. Obviously, if the whistle is made of metal, a dog can injure its mouth, teeth, or tongue. Therefore, *never* buy a "squeak toy" made with a metal whistle.

Other chew toys are made of vinyl, a cheap plastic which is

soft to the touch and pliable. Most of the cute little toys that are figures of animals or people are made of this cheap plastic. They are sometimes hand-painted in countries where the cost of such labor is low. Not only is the paint used dangerous to dogs, because of the lead content, but the vinyl tears easily and is usually destroyed by the dog during the first hour. Small bits of vinyl may be ingested and cause blockage of the intestines. You are, therefore, reminded of these things before you buy anything vinyl for your dog!

Very inexpensive dog toys, usually found in supermarkets and other low-price venues, may

*Natural chew bones can splinter and become lodged in a dog's throat. Nylon and polyurethane bones are safer for canine use.*

*Old discardable shoes should not be included in the dog's toy box. Such items are dangerous to a puppy or an adult dog.*

be made of polyethylene. These are to be avoided completely, as this cheap plastic is, for some odd reason, attractive to dogs. Dogs destroy the toy in minutes and sometimes swallow the indigestible bits and pieces that come off. Most pet shops carry only safe toys.

## WHAT TOYS ARE SAFE FOR DOGS?

**Hard Rubber** Toys made of hard rubber are usually safe for dogs, providing the toy is made of 100% hard rubber and not a compound of rubber and other materials. The rubber must be "virgin" and not re-ground from old tires, tubes, and other scrap rubber products. The main problem with rubber, even 100% virgin rubber, is that it oxidizes quickly, especially when subjected to the ultraviolet rays of the sun and a dog's saliva. The rubber then tends to be brittle, to crack, to dust off, and to be extremely dangerous to dogs that like swallowing things. **Nylon Toys** Toys made of nylon could well be the safest of all toys, *providing the nylon is annealed.* Nylon that is not annealed is very fragile, and if you smash it against a hard surface, it might shatter like glass. The same is true when the weather is cold and the nylon drops below freezing. Thus far there is only one line of dog toys that is made of annealed virgin nylon—Nylabone®. These toys not only are annealed but they are flavored and scented. The flavors and scents, such as hambone, are undetectable by humans, but dogs seem to find them attractive.

Some nylon bones have the flavor sprayed on them or molded into them. These cheaper bones are easy to detect—just smell them. If you

*The Puppy Bone® by Nylabone® is multi-purpose, designed for teething, chew-pacification, teeth-cleaning and the elimination of behavioral problems before they become habitual.*

discern an odor, you know they are poorly made. The main problem with the nylon toys that have an odor is that they are not annealed and they "smell up"

the house or car. The dog's saliva dilutes the odor of the bone, and when he drops it on your rug, this odor attaches itself to the rug and is quite difficult to remove.

Annealed nylon may be the best there is, but it is not 100% safe. The Nylabone® dog chews are really meant to be Pooch Pacifiers®. This trade name indicates the effect intended for the dog, which is to relieve the tension in your excited puppy or anxious adult dog. Instead of chewing up the furniture or some other object, he chews up his Nylabone® instead. Many dogs ignore the Nylabone® for weeks, suddenly attacking it when they have to relieve their doggie tensions.

The Nylabone® is designed for the most aggressive chewers. Even so, owners should be wary that some dogs may have jaws strong enough to chomp off a piece of Nylabone®, but this is extremely rare. *One word of caution:* the Nylabone® should be replaced when the dog has chewed down the knuckle. Most dogs slowly scrape off small slivers of nylon which pass harmlessly through their digestive tract. The resultant frizzled bone actually becomes a toothbrush.

One of the great characteristics of nylon bones is that they can be boiled and sterilized. If a dog loses interest in his Nylabone®, or it is too hard for him to chew due to his age and the condition of his teeth, you can cook it in some chicken or beef broth, allowing it to boil for 30 minutes. Let it cool down normally. It will then be perfectly sterile and re-flavored for the next dog. *Don't try this with plastic bones, as they will melt and ruin your pot.*

**Polyurethane Toys** Because polyurethane bones such as the Gumabone® are constructed of the strongest *flexible* materials known, some dogs (and their owners) actually prefer them to the traditional nylon bones. There are several brands on the market: ignore the ones which have scents that you can discern. Some of the scented polyurethane bones have an unbearable odor after the scent has rubbed off the bone and onto your rug or car seat. Again, look for the better-quality polyurethane toy. Gumabone® is a flexible material, the same as used for making artificial hearts and the bumpers on automobiles, thus it is strong and stable. It is not as strong as Nylabone®, but many dogs like it because it is soft.

If your dog is soft-mouthed and a less aggressive, more playful chewer, he will love the great taste and fun feel of the Gumabone® products.

The most popular of the

Gumabone® products made in polyurethane are the tug toys, knots, balls, and Frisbee® flying discs. These items are almost clear in color, have the decided advantage of lasting a long time, and are useful in providing exercise for both a dog and his master or mistress.

*Gumabone® is available in different sizes and shapes. These are probably the most popular of all chew toys because dogs love them.*

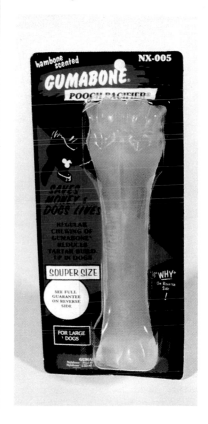

Gumabone® has also introduced new spiral-shaped dental devices under the name Plaque Attacker®. These unique products are fast becoming standards for all aggressive chewers. The Plaque Attacker Dental Device® comes in four fun sizes and each is designed to maximize gum and teeth

Attacker® products are patented and scented with hambone to make them even more enticing for the dog. Clinical findings support the assertion that a significant reduction in calculus accompanies use of the Gumbone® products.

Whatever dog toy you buy, be sure it is high quality. Pet shops

*The Plaque Attacker® is a Dental Ball™, not just a plaything, designed to reduce plaque and tartar by use of its revolutionary "dental tips."*

massage through its upraised "dental tips," which pimple the surface of the toy. Similarly, the Plaque Attacker Dental Ball® ensures a reduction in plaque and tartar. This one-of-a-kind product provides hours of fun for a dog. It bounces erratically and proves to be the most exciting of all polyurethane toys. All Plaque

and certain supermarkets, as a rule, always carry the better quality toys. Of course there may be exceptions, but you are best advised to ask your local pet shop operator—or even your veterinarian—what toys are suitable for *your* dog.

In conclusion, if your dog is a swallower of foreign objects,

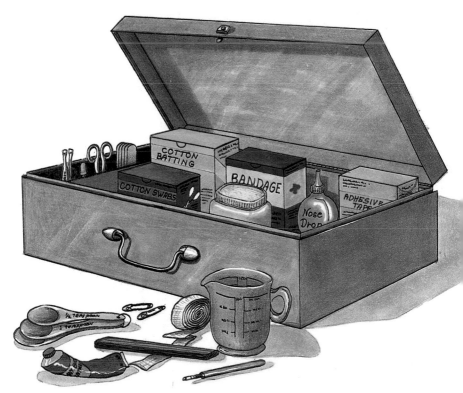

*When emergencies occur, being prepared pays off. A first-aid kit should be accessible and always well stocked with medical accessories and supplies.*

don't give him anything cheap to chew on. If he swallows a coin, you can hardly blame the Treasury! Unless your dog is carefully supervised, use only the largest size Nylabone® and Gumabone®, and replace them as soon as the dog chews down the knuckles. *Do not let the dog take the Nylabone® outdoors.* First of all he can hide and bury it, digging it up when his tensions rise. Then, too, all nylon becomes more brittle when it freezes, even Nylabone®.

## IF YOUR PET SWALLOWS POISON

A poisoned dog must be treated instantly; any delay could cause his death. Different poisons act in different ways and require different treatments. If you know the dog has swallowed an acid, alkali, gasoline, or kerosene, do not induce vomiting. Give milk to dilute the poison and rush him to the vet. If you can find the bottle or container of poison, check the label to see if there is a recommended antidote. If not, try to induce vomiting by giving him a mixture of hydrogen peroxide and water. Mix the regular drugstore strength of hydrogen peroxide (3%) with an equal part of water, but do not attempt to pour it down your dog's throat, as that could cause inhalation pneumonia. Instead, simply pull the dog's lips away from the side of his mouth, making a pocket for depositing the liquid. Use at least a tablespoonful of the mixture for every ten pounds of your dog's

weight. He will vomit in about two minutes. When his stomach has settled, give him a teaspoonful of Epsom salts in a little water to empty the intestine quickly. The hydrogen peroxide, on ingestion, becomes oxygen and water and is harmless to your dog; it is the best antidote for phosphorus, which is often used in rat poisons. After you have administered this emergency treatment to your pet and his stomach and bowels have been emptied, rush him to your veterinarian for further care.

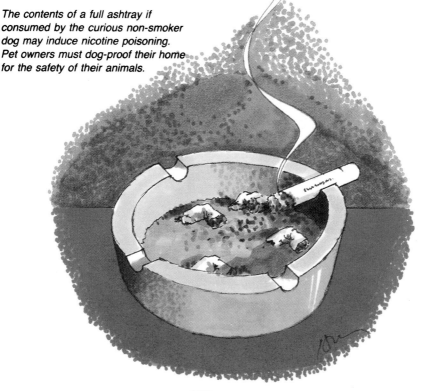

*The contents of a full ashtray if consumed by the curious non-smoker dog may induce nicotine poisoning. Pet owners must dog-proof their home for the safety of their animals.*

## DANGER IN THE HOME

There are numerous household products that can prove fatal if ingested by your pet. These include rat poison, antifreeze, boric acid, hand soap, detergents, insecticides, mothballs, household cleansers, bleaches, de-icers, polishes and disinfectants, paint and varnish removers, acetone, turpentine, and even health and beauty aids

There is another danger lurking within the home among the household plants, which are almost all poisonous, even if swallowed in small quantities. There are hundreds of poisonous plants around us, among which are: ivy leaves, cyclamen, lily of the valley, rhododendrons, tulip bulbs, azalea, wisteria, poinsettia leaves, mistletoe, daffodils,

if ingested in large enough quantities. A word to the wise should be sufficient: what you would keep locked away from your two-year-old child should also be kept hidden from your pet.

*Preparing for emergencies also requires that an owner understand such basic revival techniques as cardio-pulmonary resuscitation, chest compression, heart massage, heat stroke measures, and many others.*

*Checking for an animal's vital signs in the event of an emergency will help you to provide the veterinarian with the answers to his preliminary questions.*

jimson weed—we cannot name them all. Rhubarb leaves, for example, either raw or cooked, can cause death or violent convulsions. Peach, elderberry, and cherry trees can cause cyanide poisoning if their bark is consumed.

There are also many insects that can be poisonous to dogs such as spiders, bees, wasps, and some flies. A few toads and frogs exude a fluid that can make a dog foam at the mouth—and even kill him—if he bites too hard!

There have been cases of dogs suffering nicotine poisoning by consuming the contents of full ashtrays which thoughtless smokers have left on the coffee table. Also, do not leave nails, staples, pins, or other sharp objects lying around. Likewise, don't let your puppy play with plastic bags which could suffocate him. Unplug, remove, or cover any electrical cords or wires near your dog. Chewing live wires could lead to severe mouth burns or death. Remember that an ounce of prevention is worth a pound of cure: keep all potentially dangerous objects out of your pet's reach.

## VEHICLE TRAVEL SAFETY

A dog should never be left alone in a car. It takes only a few minutes for the heat to become unbearable in the summer, and to drop to freezing in the winter.

A dog traveling in a car or truck should be well behaved. An undisciplined dog can be deadly in a moving vehicle. The dog should be trained to lie on the back seat of the vehicle. Allowing your dog to stick its head out of the window is unwise. The dog may jump or it may get something in its eye. Some manufacturers sell seat belts and car seats designed for dogs.

Traveling with your dog in the back of your pick-up truck is an unacceptable notion and dangerous to all involved.

## PROTECT YOURSELF FIRST

In almost all first aid situations, the dog is in pain. He may indeed be in shock and not appear to be suffering, until you move him. Then he may bite your hand or resist being helped at all. So if you want to help your dog, help yourself first by tying his mouth closed. To do this, use a piece of strong cloth four inches wide and three feet long, depending on the size of the dog.

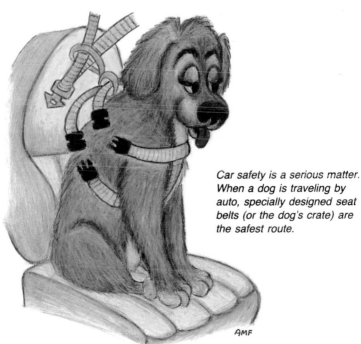

*Car safety is a serious matter. When a dog is traveling by auto, specially designed seat belts (or the dog's crate) are the safest route.*

AMF

Make a loop in the middle of the strip and slip it over his nose with the knot under his chin and over the bony part of his nose. Pull it tight and bring the ends back around his head behind the ears and tie it tightly, ending with a bow knot for quick, easy release. Now you can handle the dog safely. As a dog perspires through his tongue, do not leave the "emergency muzzle" on any longer than necessary.

## ADMINISTERING MEDICINE

When you are giving liquid medicine to your dog, it is a good idea to pull the lips away from the side of the mouth, form a lip pocket, and let the liquid trickle past the tongue. Remain at his side, never in front of the dog, as he may cough and spray you with the liquid. Moreover, you must never pour liquid medicine while the victim's tongue is drawn out, as

*First aid, in the ideal sense, is the temporary care of an animal or person until professional help can be found. Recognizing the urgency in any given circumstance is the primary concern. Moving an injured animal with utmost care usually requires two persons and a clean blanket.*

inhalation pneumonia could be the disastrous result.

Medicine in pill form is best administered by forcing the dog's mouth open, holding his forced to swallow the medicine. As the dog will not be feeling well, stroke his neck to comfort him and to help him swallow his medicine more easily. Do keep

*Before attempting to transport an injured dog, be very careful to inspect for apparent wounds, burns or breaks while disturbing the animal as little as possible. Laying the dog in a flat position will make the carrying easier to manage.*

head back, and placing the capsule as far back on his tongue as you can reach. To do this: put the palm of your hand over the dog's muzzle (his foreface) with your fingers on one side of his jaw, your thumb on the other. Press his lips hard against his teeth while using your other hand to pull down his lower jaw. With your two fingers, try to put the pill as far back on the dog's tongue as you can reach. Keep his mouth and nostrils closed and he should be an eye on him for a few moments afterward, however, to make certain that he does not spit it out.

## IN CASE OF AN ACCIDENT

It is often difficult for you to assess the dog's injuries after a road accident. He may appear normal, but there might be internal hemorrhaging. A vital organ could be damaged or ribs broken. Keep the dog as quiet and warm as possible; cover him with blankets or your coat to let his own body heat build up. Signs of shock are a rapid and weak pulse, glassy-eyed appearance, subnormal temperature, and slow capillary refill time. To determine the last symptom, press firmly against the dog's gums until they turn white. Release and count the number of seconds until the gums return to their normal color. If it is more than 2–3 seconds, the dog may be going into shock. Failure to return to the reddish pink color indicates that the dog may be in serious trouble and needs immediate assistance.

If artificial respiration is required, first open the dog's mouth and check for obstructions; extend his tongue and examine the pharynx. Clear his mouth of mucus and blood and hold the mouth slightly open. Mouth-to-mouth resuscitation involves holding the dog's tongue to the bottom of his mouth with one hand and sealing his nostrils with the other while you blow into his mouth. Watch for his chest to rise with each inflation. Repeat every 5–6 seconds, the equivalent of 10–12 breaths a minute.

If the veterinarian cannot come to you, try to improvise a stretcher to take the dog to him. To carry a puppy, wrap him in a blanket that has been folded into several thicknesses. If he is in shock, it is better to pick him up by holding one hand under his chest, the other under the hindquarters. This will keep him stretched out.

It is always better to roll an injured dog than to try and lift him. If you find him lying beside the road after a car accident, apply a muzzle even if you have to use someone's necktie to make one. Send someone for a blanket and roll him gently onto it. Two people, one on each side, can make a stretcher out of the blanket and move the dog easily.

If no blanket is available and the injured dog must be moved, try to keep him as flat as possible. So many dogs' backs are broken in car accidents that one must first consider that possibility. However, if he can move his hind legs or tail, his spine is probably not broken. Get medical assistance for him immediately.

It should be mentioned that unfortunate car accidents, which can maim or kill your dog, can be avoided if he is confined at all times either indoors or, if out-of-doors, in a fenced-in yard or some other protective enclosure. *Never* allow your dog to roam free; even a well-trained dog may, for some unknown reason, dart into the street—and the result could be tragic.

If you need to walk your dog, leash him first so that he will be protected from moving vehicles.

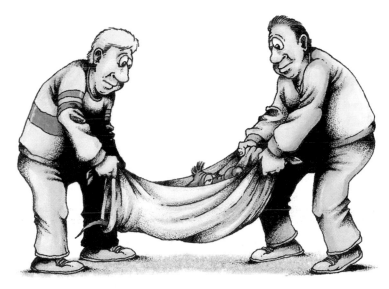

*It is the smooth, efficient execution of first-aid technique that saves lives. Costly mistakes happen when haste and frenzy take over. When moving an injured dog, keep calm and be focused on the situation at hand. Act swiftly and maintain control at all times.*

## PROTECTING YOUR PET

It is important to watch for any tell-tale signs of illness so that you can spare your pet any unnecessary suffering. Your dog's eyes, for example, should normally be bright and alert, so if the haw is bloodshot or partially covers the eye, it may be a sign of illness or irritation. If your dog has matter in the corners of his eyes, bathe them with a mild eye wash; obtain ointment or eye drops from your veterinarian to treat a chronic condition.

If your dog seems to have something wrong with his ears which causes him to scratch at them or shake his head, cautiously probe the ear with a cotton swab. An accumulation of wax will probably work itself out. Dirt or dried blood, however, is indicative of ear mites or infection and should be treated immediately. Sore ears in the summer, due to insect bites, should be washed with mild soap and water, then covered with a soothing ointment and wrapped in gauze if necessary. Keep your pet away from insects until his ears heal, even if this means confining him indoors.

## VACCINATION SCHEDULE

| Age | Vaccination |
|---|---|
| 6-8 weeks | Initial canine distemper, canine hepatitis, tracheobronchitis, canine parvovirus, as well as initial leptospirosis vaccination. |
| 10-12 weeks | Second vaccination for all given at 6-8 weeks. Initial rabies and initial Lyme disease to be given at this time. |
| 14-16 weeks | Third vaccination for all given at 6-8 and 10-12 weeks.Re-vaccinate annually, hereafter. Second rabies and second Lyme disease to be given at this time, and then re-vaccinated annually. |

**INOCULATIONS**

Periodic check-ups by your veterinarian throughout your puppy's life are good health insurance. The person from whom your puppy was purchased should tell you what inoculations your puppy has had and when the next visit to the vet is necessary. You must make certain that your puppy has been vaccinated against the following infectious canine diseases: distemper, canine hepatitis, leptospirosis, rabies, parvovirus, and parainfluenza. Annual "boosters" thereafter provide inexpensive protection for your dog against such serious diseases. Puppies should also be checked for worms at an early age.

*Vaccination schedules should be confirmed with your vet.*

**DISTEMPER**

Young dogs are most susceptible to distemper, although it may affect dogs of all ages. Some signs of the disease are loss of appetite, depression, chills, and fever, as well as a watery discharge from the eyes and nose. Unless treated promptly, the disease goes into advanced stages with infections of the lungs, intestines, and nervous system. Dogs that recover may be impaired with paralysis, convulsions, a twitch, or some other defect, usually spastic in nature. Early inoculations in puppyhood should be followed by an annual booster to help protect against this disease.

## CANINE HEPATITIS

The signs of hepatitis are drowsiness, loss of appetite, high temperature, and great thirst. These signs may be accompanied by swellings of the head, neck, and abdomen. Vomiting may also occur. This disease strikes quickly, and death may occur in only a few hours. An annual booster shot is needed after the initial series of puppy shots.

## LEPTOSPIROSIS

Infection caused by either of two serovars, *canicola* or *copehageni,* is usually begun by the dog's licking substances contaminated by the urine or feces of infected animals. Brown rats are the main carriers of *copehageni.* The signs are weakness, vomiting, and a yellowish discoloration of the jaws, teeth, and tongue, caused by an inflammation of the kidneys. A veterinarian can administer the bacterins to protect your dog from this disease. The frequency of the doses is determined by the risk factor involved.

## RABIES

This disease of the dog's central nervous system spreads by infectious saliva, which is

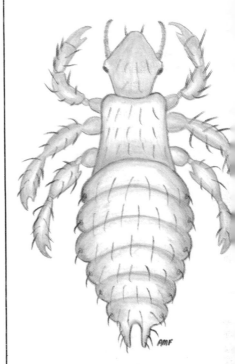

Lice are not a common problem in dogs and usually only infest dogs that are poorly cared for. Proper care of your dog will prevent lice infestation.

transmitted by the bite of an infected animal. Of the two main classes of signs, the first is "furious rabies," in which the dog shows a period of melancholy or depression, then irritation, and finally paralysis. The first period can be from a few hours to several days, and during this time the dog is cross and will change his position often, lose his appetite, begin to lick, and bite or swallow foreign objects. During this phase the dog is spasmodically wild and has impulses to run away. The dog acts fearless and bites everything in sight. If he is caged or confined, he will fight at the bars and possibly break teeth or fracture his jaw. His bark

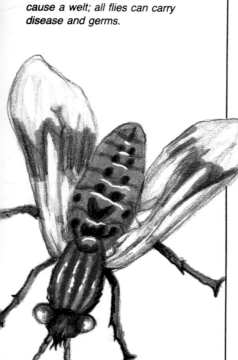

*The deer fly has a wicked bite that can cause a welt; all flies can carry disease and germs.*

becomes a peculiar howl. In the final stage, the animal's lower jaw becomes paralyzed and hangs down. He then walks with a stagger, and saliva drips from his mouth. About four to eight days after the onset of paralysis, the dog dies.

The second class of symptoms is referred to as "dumb rabies" and is characterized by the dog's walking in a bearlike manner with his head down. The lower jaw is paralyzed and the dog is unable to bite. It appears as if he has a bone caught in his throat.

If a dog is bitten by a rabid animal, he probably can be saved if he is taken to a veterinarian in time for a series of injections. After the signs appear, however, no cure is possible. The local health department must be notified in the case of a rabid dog, for he is a danger to all who come near him. As with the other shots each year, an annual rabies inoculation is very important. In many areas, the administration of rabies vaccines for dogs is required by law.

## PARVOVIRUS

This relatively new virus is a contagious disease that has spread in almost epidemic proportions throughout certain sections of the United States. It has also appeared in Australia, Canada, and Europe. Canine parvovirus attacks the intestinal tract, white blood cells, and heart muscle. It is believed to spread through dog-to-dog contact, and the specific course of infection seems to come from fecal matter of infected dogs. Overcoming parvovirus is difficult, for it is capable of existing in the environment for many months under varying conditions and temperatures, and it can be transmitted from place to place on the hair and feet of infected dogs, as well as on the clothes and shoes of people.

Vomiting and severe diarrhea, which will appear within five to seven days after the animal has been exposed to the virus, are the initial signs of this disease. At the onset of illness, feces will be light gray or yellow-gray in color, and the urine might be blood-streaked. Because of the vomiting and severe diarrhea, the dog that has contracted the disease will dehydrate quickly. Depression and loss of appetite, as well as a rise in temperature, can accompany the other symptoms. Death caused by this disease usually occurs within 48 to 72 hours following the appearance of the symptoms. Puppies are hardest hit, and the virus is fatal to 75 percent of puppies that contract it. Death in puppies can be within two days of the onset of the illness.

A series of shots administered by a veterinarian is the best

The stable fly is capable of a painful bite.

preventive measure for canine parvovirus. It is also important to disinfect the area where the dog is housed by using one part sodium hypochlorite solution (household bleach) to thirty parts of water and to keep the dog from coming into contact with the fecal matter of other dogs.

### LYME DISEASE

Known as a bacterial infection, Lyme disease is transmitted by ticks infected with a spirochete known as *Borrelia burgdorferi*. The disease is most often

The deer tick is a principal carrier of Lyme disease.

The brown dog tick is the most common tick found on dogs. It is much larger than a deer tick.

acquired by the parasitic bite of an infected deer tick, *Ixodes dammini*. While the range of symptoms is broad, common warning signs include: rash beginning at the bite and soon extending in a bullseye-targetlike fashion; chills, fever, lack of balance, lethargy, and stiffness; swelling and pain, especially in the joints, possibly leading to arthritis or arthritic conditions; heart problems, weak limbs, facial paralysis, and lack of tactile sensation.

Concerned dog owners, especially those living in the United States, should contact a veterinarian to discuss Lyme disease. A vaccination has been developed and is routinely administered to puppies twice before the 16th week, and then annually.

## PARAINFLUENZA

Parainfluenza, or infectious canine tracheobronchitis, is commonly known as "kennel cough." It is highly contagious, affects the upper respiratory system, and is spread through direct or indirect contact with already diseased dogs. It will readily infect dogs of all ages that have not been vaccinated or that were previously infected. While this condition is definitely one of the serious diseases in dogs, it is self-limiting, usually lasting only two to four weeks.

The symptoms are high fever and intense, harsh coughing that brings up mucus. As long as your pet sees your veterinarian immediately, the chances for his complete recovery are excellent.

## EXTERNAL PARASITES

A parasite is an animal that lives in or on an organism of another species, known as the host, without contributing to the well-being of the host. The majority of dogs' skin problems are parasitic in nature and an estimated 90% of puppies are born with parasites.

Ticks can cause serious problems to dogs where the latter have access to woods, fields, and vegetation in which large numbers of native mammals live. Ticks are usually found clinging to vegetation and attach themselves to animals passing by. They have eight legs and a heavy shield or shell-like covering on their upper surface. Only by keeping dogs away from tick-infested areas can ticks on dogs be prevented.

The flea is the single most common cause of skin and coat problems in dogs. There are 11,000 kinds of fleas which can transmit specific disorders like tapeworm and heartworm or transport smaller parasites onto your dog. The common tapeworm, for example, requires the flea as an intermediate host for completion of its life cycle.

*Fumigating flea bombs are commonly used to de-flea a home. It is essential to follow the manufacturer's instructions to the letter, as this product's fumes can kill more than just insects.*

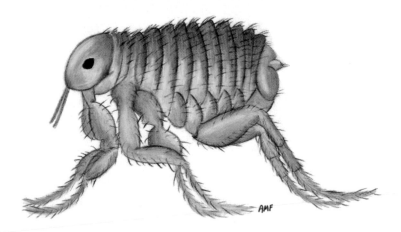

A female flea can lay hundreds of eggs and these will become adults in less than three weeks. Depending on the temperature and the amount of moisture, large numbers of fleas can attack dogs. The ears of dogs, in particular, can play host to hundreds of fleas.

Fleas can lurk in crevices and cracks, carpets, and bedding for months, so frequent cleaning of your dog's environment is absolutely essential. If he is infected by other dogs, then have him bathed and "dipped," which means that he will be put into water containing a chemical that kills fleas. Your veterinarian will advise which dip to use, and your dog must be bathed for at least twenty minutes. These parasites are tenacious and remarkably agile creatures; fleas have existed since prehistoric times and have been found in arctic as well as tropical

*Fleas are among the most common external parasites and can be real pests to eliminate from your pet.*

climates. Some experts claim that fleas can jump 150 times the length of their bodies; this makes them difficult to catch and kill. Thus, treating your pet for parasites without simultaneously treating the environment is both inefficient and ineffective.

## INTERNAL PARASITES

Four common internal parasites that may infect a dog are: roundworms, hookworms, whipworms, and tapeworms. The first three can be diagnosed by laboratory examination of the dog's stool, and tapeworms can be seen in the stool or attached to the hair around the anus. When a veterinarian determines what type of worm or worms are present, he then can advise the best treatment.

Roundworms, the dog's most common intestinal parasite, have a life cycle which permits complete eradication by worming twice, ten days apart. The first worming will remove all adults and the second will destroy all subsequently hatched eggs before they, in turn, can produce more parasites.

A dog in good physical condition is less susceptible to worm infestation than a weak dog. Proper sanitation and a nutritious diet help in preventing worms. One of the best preventive measures is to have clean, dry bedding for the dog, as this diminishes the possibility of reinfection due to flea or tick bites.

Heartworm infestation in dogs is passed by mosquitoes. Dogs with this disease tire easily, have difficulty in breathing, and lose weight despite a hearty appetite. Administration of preventive medicine throughout the spring, summer, and fall months is advised. A veterinarian must first take a blood sample from the dog to test for the presence of the disease, and if the dog is heartworm-free, pills or liquid medicine can be prescribed to protect against any infestation.

## CANINE SENIOR CITIZENS

The processes of aging and gradual degenerative changes start far earlier in a dog than often observed, usually at about seven years of age. If we recall that each year of a dog's life roughly corresponds to about seven years in the life of a man,

*The fraternity of internal parasites and their eggs: whipworms, hookworms, roundworms and tapeworms.*

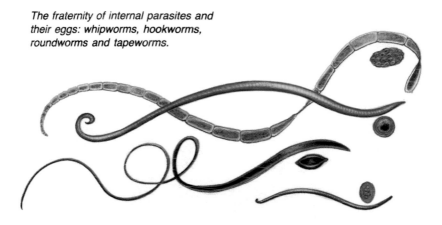

by the age of seven he is well into middle age. Your pet will become less active, will have a poorer appetite with increased thirst, there will be frequent periods of constipation and less than normal passage of urine. His skin and coat might become dull and dry and his hair will become thin and fall out. There is a tendency towards obesity in old age, which should be avoided by maintaining a regular exercise program. Remember, also, that your pet will be less able to cope with extreme heat, cold, fatigue, and change in routine.

There is the possibility of loss or impairment of hearing or eyesight. He may become bad-tempered more often than in the past. Other ailments such as rheumatism, arthritis, kidney infections, heart disease, male prostatism, and hip dysplasia may occur. Of course, all these require a veterinarian's examination and recommendation of suitable treatment. Care of the teeth is

*Heartworm life cycle: a carrier mosquito bites a dog and deposits microfilariae, which travel through the dog's bloodstream, lodging in the heart to reproduce. The carrier dog is later bitten by an uninfected mosquito, which becomes infected, and bites and infects another dog . . . .*

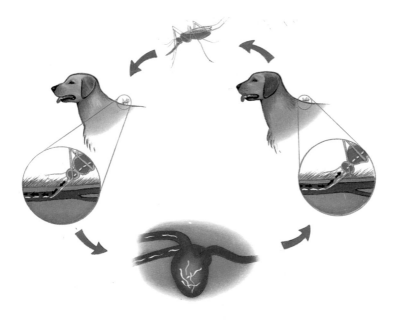

*Taking a dog's pulse is useful as it reflects his heartbeat. To do so is quite simple: feel along the inside of your dog's thigh at the juncture where it meets the body. Press with a finger to feel the pulsation. (Do not use your thumb.)*

also important in the aging dog. Indeed, the mouth can be a barometer of nutritional health. Degenerating gums, heavy tartar on the teeth, loose teeth, and sore lips are common. The worst of all diseases in old age, however, is neglect. Good care in early life will have its effect on your dog's later years; the nutrition and general health care of his first few years can determine his lifespan and the quality of his life. It is worth bearing in mind that the older, compared to the younger, animal needs more protein of good biological value, more vitamins A, B-complex, D and E, more calcium and iron, and less fat.

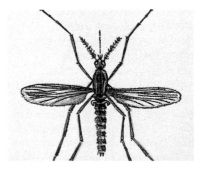

*An adult male mosquito. Only female mosquitoes will suck blood from a host animal.*

# Preventive Dental Care

## ALL DOGS NEED TO CHEW

Puppies and young dogs need something with resistance to chew on while their teeth and jaws are developing—to cut the puppy teeth, to induce growth of the permanent teeth under the puppy teeth, to assist in getting

*An artist's representation of the calculus index, ranging from index rating* **4** *(topmost drawing) through index rating* **0** *(lowest drawing).*

**4** *Buccal crown covered*

**3** *⅔ crown covered*

**2** *⅓ crown covered*

**1** *Only gingival margin covered*

**0** *No calculus evident*

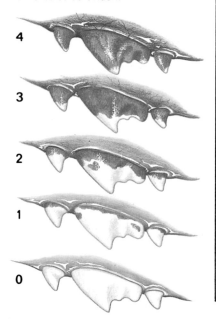

4

3

2

1

0

rid of the puppy teeth on time, to help the permanent teeth through the gums, to assure normal jaw development and to settle the permanent teeth solidly in the jaws.

The adult dog's desire to chew stems from the instinct for tooth cleaning, gum massage, and jaw exercise—plus the need to vent periodic doggie tensions. . . . A pacifier if you will!

Dental caries, as they affect the teeth of humans, are virtually unknown in dogs; but tartar (calculus) accumulates on the teeth of dogs, particularly at the gum line, more rapidly than on the teeth of humans. These accumulations, if not removed, bring irritation and then infection, which erode the tooth enamel and ultimately destroy the teeth at the roots. It is important that you take your dog to your local veterinarian for periodic dental examinations.

Tooth and jaw development will normally continue until the dog is more than a year old—but sometimes much longer, depending upon the dog, its chewing exercise, rate of calcium utilization and many other factors, known and unknown, which affect the development of individual dogs. Diseases, like distemper for example, may sometimes arrest development of the teeth and jaws, which may resume months or even years later.

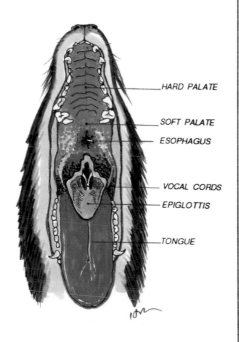

HARD PALATE

SOFT PALATE

ESOPHAGUS

VOCAL CORDS

EPIGLOTTIS

TONGUE

*The owner should inspect the dog's mouth regularly to check that all is well.*

This is why dogs, especially puppies and young dogs, will often destroy valuable property when their chewing instinct is not diverted from their owners' possessions, particularly during the widely varying critical period for young dogs. Saving your possessions from destruction, assuring proper development of

teeth and jaws, providing for "interim" tooth cleaning and gum massage, and channeling doggie tensions into a non-destructive outlet are, therefore, all dependent upon the dog's having something suitable for chewing readily available when his instinct tells him to chew. If your purposes, and those of your dog, are to be accomplished, what you provide for chewing must be desirable from the doggie viewpoint, have the necessary functional qualities, and, above all, be safe.

It is very important that dogs be prohibited from chewing on anything they can break or indigestible things from which they can bite sizeable chunks. Sharp pieces, such as those from a bone which can be broken by a dog, may pierce the intestinal wall and kill. Indigestible things which can be bitten off in chunks, such as toys made of rubber compound or cheap plastic, may cause an intestinal stoppage; if not regurgitated, they are certain to bring painful death unless surgery is promptly performed.

## NATURAL CHEW BONES

Strong natural bones, such as 4- to 8-inch lengths of round shin bone from mature beef—either the kind you can get from your butcher or one of the varieties available commercially in pet stores—may serve your dog's teething needs, if his mouth is large enough to handle them.

You may be tempted to give your puppy a smaller bone and he may not be able to break it when you do, but puppies grow rapidly and the power of their jaws constantly increases until maturity. This means that a growing dog may break one of

excessive chewing on animal bones. Contrary to popular belief, knuckle bones that can be chewed up and swallowed by the dog provide little, if any, useable calcium or other nutrient. They do, however, disturb the digestion of most dogs and might cause them to vomit the nourishing food they really need.

*Rawhide treats are enjoyed by dogs. Owners should be wary since rawhide can tear off in large pieces and lodge in the dog's throat or cause intestinal blockage.*

the smaller bones at any time, swallow the pieces and die painfully before you realize what is wrong.

All hard natural bones are highly abrasive. If your dog is an avid chewer, natural bones may wear away his teeth prematurely; hence, they then should be taken away from your dog when the teething purposes have been served. The badly worn, and usually painful, teeth of many mature dogs can be traced to

### RAWHIDE CHEWS

The most popular material from which dog chews are made is the hide from cows, horses, and other animals. Most of these chews are made in foreign countries where the quality of the hide is not good enough for making leather. These foreign hides may contain lead, antibiotics, arsenic, or insecticides which might be detrimental to the health of your dog . . . or even your children. It is not impossible that a small child will start chewing on a piece of rawhide meant for the dog! Rawhide chews do not serve the primary chewing functions very well. They are also a bit messy when wet from mouthing, and most dogs chew them up rather rapidly. They have been considered safe for dogs until recently.

Rawhide is flavorful to dogs. They like it. Currently, some veterinarians have been attributing cases of acute constipation to large pieces of incompletely digested rawhide in the intestine. Basically it is good for them to chew on, but dogs think rawhide is food. They do not play with it nor do they use it as a pacifier to relieve doggie tension. They eat it as they would any other food. This is dangerous, for the hide is very difficult for dogs to digest and swallow, and many dogs choke on large particles of rawhide that become stuck in their throats. *Before you offer your dog rawhide chews, consult your veterinarian.* Vets have a lot of experience with canine chewing devices; ask them what they recommend.

*Annealed nylon and polyurethane chew toys are recommended by veterinarians as proven-safe and effective canine chew devices.*

## NYLON CHEW DEVICES

The nylon bones, especially those with natural meat and bone flavor added, are probably the most complete, safe, and economical answer to the chewing need. Dogs cannot break them nor bite off sizeable chunks; hence, they are completely safe. And being longer lasting than other things offered for the purpose, they are very economical.

Hard chewing raises little bristle-like projections on the surface of the nylon bones to provide effective interim tooth

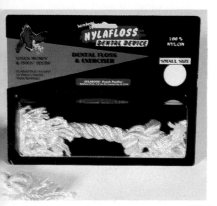

*The Nylafloss® cannot cure tooth decay, but it is an optimum decay-prevention device. Make your dog's playtime a healthy time and invest in your pet's future.*

cleaning and vigorous gum massage, much in the same way your toothbrush does it for you. The little projections are raked off and swallowed in the form of thin shavings, but the chemistry of the nylon is such that they break down in the stomach fluids and pass through without effect.

The toughness of the nylon provides the strong chewing resistance needed for important jaw exercise and effective help for the teething functions; however, there is no tooth wear because nylon is non-abrasive. Being inert, nylon does not support the growth of microorganisms, and it can be washed in soap and water or sterilized by boiling or in an autoclave.

There are a great variety of Nylabone® products available that veterinarians recommend as safe and healthy for your dog or puppy to chew on. These Nylabone® Pooch Pacifiers® usually don't splinter, chip, or break off in large chunks; instead, they are frizzled by the dog's chewing action, and this creates a toothbrush-like surface that cleanses the teeth and massages the gums. At the same time, these hard-nylon therapeutic devices channel doggie tension and chewing frustation into constructive rather than destructive behavior. The original nylon bone (Nylabone®) is not a toy and dogs use it only when in need of pacification. Keeping a bone in each of your dog's recreation rooms is the best method of providing the requisite pacification. Unfortunately, many nylon chew products have been copied. These inferior quality copies are sold in supermarkets and other chain stores. The really good products are sold only through veterinarians, pet shops, grooming salons and places where the sales people really know something about dogs. The good products have the flavor impregnated *into* the bone. This makes the taste last longer. The smell is undetectable to humans. The artificial bones which have a strong odor are poor-quality bones with the odor sprayed on to impress the dog owner (not the dog)! These heavily scented dog toys may impart the odor to your carpets or furniture if an odor-sprayed bone lies there wet from a dog's chewing on it.

revolutionary product that is designed to save dogs teeth and keep them healthy. Even though your dogs won't believe you, Nylafloss® is not a toy but rather a most effective agent in removing destructive plaque

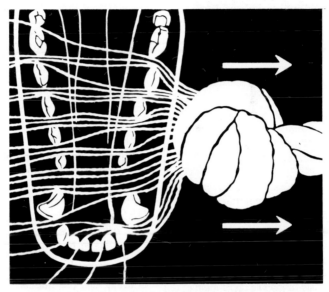

*Food particles can be deposited between the teeth, where they can be difficult to remove. Many chew products cannot work to remove these decaying food pieces. For this reason, the Nylafloss® dental device is recommended by professionals as it is the only available mechanism to clean between the dog's teeth.*

## FLOSS OR LOSS!

Most dentists relay that brushing daily is just not enough. In order to prevent unnecessary tooth loss, flossing is essential. For dogs, human dental floss is not the answer—however, canine dental devices are available. The Nylafloss® is a

between the teeth and *beneath* the gum line where gum disease begins. Gentle tugging is all that is necessary to activate the Nylafloss®. These 100% inert nylon products are guaranteed to outlast rawhide chews by ten times and are available for sale at all pet shops.

### THE IMPORTANCE OF PREVENTION

In order to get to the root of canine dentistry problems, it is important for owners to realize that no less than 75% of all canine dental health problems, serious enough to require a vet's assistance, and nearly 98% of all canine teeth lost are attributable to periodontal disease.

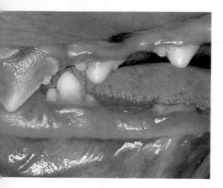

*A dog's teeth showing moderate calculus build-up. The moderate calculus build-up on this dog's teeth reflects a certain neglect by the owner. Providing a safe chew item like the Gumabone® can save your dog's teeth.*

Periodontal disease not only mars the teeth but also the gums and other buccal tissue in the mouth. Severe cases of periodontal disease involve resultant bacterial toxins which are absorbed into the blood stream and cause permanent damage to the heart and kidneys. In the infected mouth,

teeth are loosened; tartar, unsightly and bad smelling, accumulates heavily; and the dog experiences a complete loss of appetite. Long-standing periodontitis can also manifest itself in simple symptoms such as diarrhea and vomiting.

Periodontal disease deserves the attention of every dog owner—a dog's teeth are extremely important to his ongoing health. The accumulation of plaque, food matter mixed with saliva attaching itself to the tooth surface, is a sure sign of potential bacteria build-up. As toxic material gathers, the bone surrounding the teeth erodes. If plaque and calculus continue to reside without attention, bacteria-fighting cells will form residual pus at the root of the teeth, dividing the gum from the tooth. The debris is toxic and actually kills the buccal tissue. This is a most undesirable situation, as hardened dental calculus is one of the most direct causative agents of periodontitis.

In actuality, the disease is a result of a number of contributing factors. Old age, a diet comprised solely of soft or semi-soft foods, dental tartar, constant chewing of hair and even coprophagy (the eating of stool) are among the most common contributors.

Just as regular dental visits and brushing are necessary for humans, regular hygienic care and veterinary check-ups can help control tooth problems in canines. Involved and expensive routines can be performed on the affected, neglected mouth and teeth if decay has begun eroding the enamel and infecting the gums. Cleaning, polishing, and scaling are routine to remove calculus build-up.

Owners must claim responsibility for their dog's health, and tooth care is no small aspect of the care required. Daily brushing with a salt/baking soda solution is the best answer, but many owners find this tedious or just too difficult to perform. The simpler and more proven effective way to avoid, reduce, and fight periodontal disease and calculus build-up is giving the dog regular access to a thermoplastic polymer chew device. The Gumabone® products are the only scientifically proven line that offers the desired protection from calculus and tartar build-up.

## CANINE DENTAL BREAKTHROUGH

The independent research of Dr. Andrew Duke, D.V.M., reveals that 70% of the dogs that regularly use Gumabone® experience a reduction of calculus build-up. This find is a breakthrough for the dog world, since the Gumabone® has already resided in the toy boxes

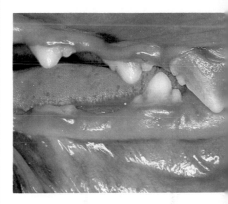

*Regular use of the Gumabone® chew products can significantly reduce plaque build-up.*

of many dogs as their favorite play item. Little did owners know previously that their dogs were gaining entertainment and unparalleled dental treatment at the same time. Dr. Duke writes: "There is little debate left that dental calculus is an excellent

*Teeth of an infected dog showing little to no plaque accumulation after professional cleaning.*

# Preventive Dental Care

indicator of periodontal health in the dog, just as it is in humans. "Calculus does not cause gingivitis and periodontitis, but the plaque and bacteria that cause periodontitis are responsible for the mineral precipitation we know as 'calculus.' All veterinarians who have made a study of dogs' oral health have noticed the middle aged dog who actively chews with excellent gingival health. Many of these dogs that chew hard substances regularly wear the cusps down and even may expose the pulp cavity faster

than secondary dentin can be formed. Often these "excellent chewers" are presented with slab fractures of the premolars or apical abcesses.

"The challenge then becomes to find a substance which is effective in removing calculus and plaque but does not wear the enamel excessively. In an attempt to duplicate the chewstuffs enjoyed by dogs in the wild, researchers have used bovine tracheas to demonstrate the inhibition of plaque and gingivitis. Very little else has been done in veterinary medicine

*The clean healthy teeth that are desired in dogs should inspire owners to work towards better dental hygiene.*

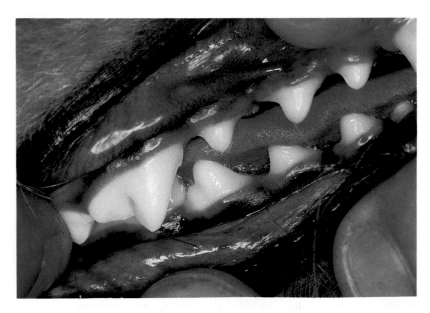

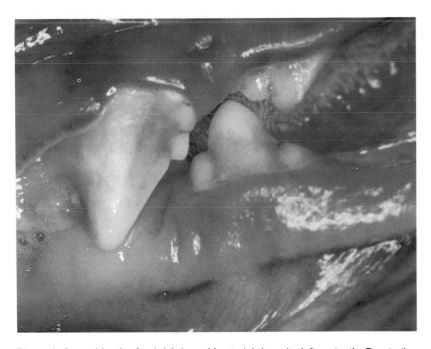

*Plaque is formed by the food debris and bacterial deposits left on teeth. Due to the high carbon dioxide and pH levels in the mouth, minerals precipitate quickly on the plaque to form calculus.*

to establish a scientific basis for evaluating chewstuffs.

"In the human field it is generally accepted (incorrectly) that fibrous foodstuffs and diet have no effect on oral health. This is a moot point since the practice of brushing is by far a more efficient technique of preventing plaque accumulation, calculus and periodontal disease. Studies in human subjects failed to find any benefits in eating apples, raw carrots, etc. If people are not allowed to brush, it is difficult to conduct clinical trials of more than one week.

"The increased awareness of animals' dental health of recent years has resulted in most veterinary practitioners' recommending some kind of chewstuff to their dog owners. To meet this market demand, there has been a stampede into the market by vendors ready to promote their products. The

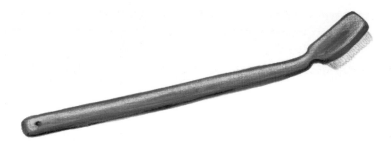

Canine tooth brushes are designed to allow access to the most hard-to-reach places in the canine mouth.

veterinarian is furnished no scientific data, but is asked to promote rawhide, bounce, and squeaky toys. How would our human colleagues handle this situation? Can Listerine® say that it prevents colds, but not support the claim? Can "Tartar Control Crest®" or "Colgate Tartar Control Formula®" be sold if it is not proven that it does in fact reduce tartar? Of course not.

"To this end, the following study was made.

"*Method:* Twenty dogs of different breeds and age were selected from a veterinary

In cases of bad neglect, scaling a dog's teeth can help to save or salvage affected teeth. Your veterinarian will perform this procedure.

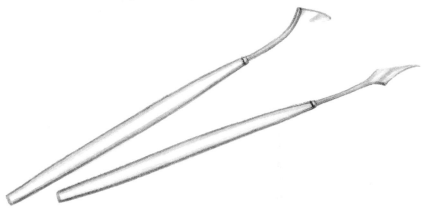

## CUMULATIVE CALCULUS INDEX SCORES

| Dog | Without Gumabone® | With Gumabone® | Difference |
|-----|-------------------|----------------|------------|
| 1. | 20 | 9 | 11 |
| 2. | 19 | 23 | - 4 |
| 3. | 49 | 26 | 23 |
| 4. | 21 | 15 | 6 |
| 5. | 34 | 11 | 23 |
| 6. | 36 | 21 | 15 |
| 7. | 44 | 31 | 13 |
| 8. | 25 | 25 | 0 |
| 9. | 34 | 28 | 6 |
| 10. | 44 | 23 | 21 |
| 11. | 22 | 15 | 7 |
| 12. | 23 | 33 | -10 |
| 13. | 26 | 23 | 3 |
| 14. | 22 | 14 | 8 |
| 15. | 20 | 20 | 0 |
| 16. | 23 | 13 | 10 |
| 17. | 24 | 14 | 10 |
| 18. | 24 | 17 | 7 |
| 19. | 24 | 31 | -7 |
| 20. | 15 | 30 | -15 |

As supported by Dr. Duke's study on reducing calculus build-up, the effectiveness of a chewing device can be measured by assigning numerical values to the accumulation when the Gumabone® device is used and not used. Seventy percent of dogs chewing Gumabone® (14 out of 20 dogs) showed a reduction in calculus build-up.

practice's clientele. Although most were from multiple pet households, none were colony dogs. The owners were asked if they would allow their dogs to be anesthetized for two prophylactic cleanings which included root planing, polishing, and gingival debridement necessary to insure good oral hygiene.

"The dogs were divided into two groups of 10. Their teeth were cleaned and their calculus index converted to 0. One group was allowed only their normal dry commercial dog ration for 30 days. The other was allowed to have free choice access to Gumabone® products of the appropriate size.

"After 30 days, photoslides were made of the upper 3rd premolar, upper 4th premolar, and the lower 4th premolar on both sides of the dog's mouth. The dogs were again subjected to a prophylactic cleaning and the group reversed. After the second 30 days, photoslides were again made. A total of six teeth in each mouth were evaluated on each dog. This was 80 slides representing 240 teeth."

Fourteen out of 20 dogs (or 70%) experienced a reduction in calculus build-up by regularly using the Gumabone® product. These products are available in a variety of sizes (for different size dogs) and designed in interesting shapes: bones, balls,

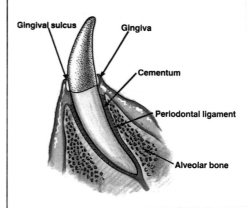

*Comparative look at healthy gums (above)* and affected gums (below) *in a dog's mouth. Instinctively dogs need to massage their gums—and the Gumabone® can satisfy this doggie craving.*

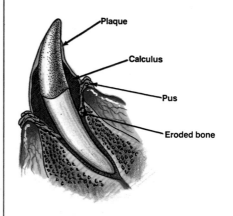

knots and rings (and even a tug toy). The entertainment value of the Gumabone® products is but an added advantage to the fighting of tooth decay and periodontitis. The products are ham-flavored and made of a thermoplastic polymer that is designed to outlast by ten times any rawhide, rubber or vinyl chew product, none of which can promise the proven benefit of the Gumabone®.

If your dog is able to chew apart a Gumabone®, it is probable that you provided him with a bone that is too small for him. Replace it with a larger one and the problem should not re-materialize. Economically, the Gumabone® is a smart choice, even without comparing it to the cost of extensive dental care.

Of course, nothing can *substitute* for periodic professional attention to your dog's teeth and gums, no more than your toothbrush can replace your dentist. Have your dog's teeth cleaned by your veterinarian at least once a year—twice a year is better—and he will be healthier, happier, and a far more pleasant companion.

Gumabones® are available through veterinarians and pet shops.

# PERPETUAL WHELPING CHART

| | 1 | 2 | 3 | 4 | 5 | 6 | 7 | 8 | 9 | 10 | 11 | 12 | 13 | 14 | 15 | 16 | 17 | 18 | 19 | 20 | 21 | 22 | 23 | 24 | 25 | 26 | 27 | 28 | 29 | 30 | 31 |
|---|---|---|---|---|---|---|---|---|---|---|---|---|---|---|---|---|---|---|---|---|---|---|---|---|---|---|---|---|---|---|---|
| Bred—Jan. | 1 | 2 | 3 | 4 | 5 | 6 | 7 | 8 | 9 | 10 | 11 | 12 | 13 | 14 | 15 | 16 | 17 | 18 | 19 | 20 | 21 | 22 | 23 | 24 | 25 | 26 | 27 | 28 | 29 | 30 | 31 |
| Due—March | 5 | 6 | 7 | 8 | 9 | 10 | 11 | 12 | 13 | 14 | 15 | 16 | 17 | 18 | 19 | 20 | 21 | 22 | 23 | 24 | 25 | 26 | 27 | 28 | 29 | 30 | 31 | April 1 | 2 | 3 | 4 |
| Bred—Feb. | 1 | 2 | 3 | 4 | 5 | 6 | 7 | 8 | 9 | 10 | 11 | 12 | 13 | 14 | 15 | 16 | 17 | 18 | 19 | 20 | 21 | 22 | 23 | 24 | 25 | 26 | 27 | 28 | | | |
| Due—April | 5 | 6 | 7 | 8 | 9 | 10 | 11 | 12 | 13 | 14 | 15 | 16 | 17 | 18 | 19 | 20 | 21 | 22 | 23 | 24 | 25 | 26 | 27 | 28 | 29 | 30 | May 1 | 2 | | | |
| Bred—Mar. | 1 | 2 | 3 | 4 | 5 | 6 | 7 | 8 | 9 | 10 | 11 | 12 | 13 | 14 | 15 | 16 | 17 | 18 | 19 | 20 | 21 | 22 | 23 | 24 | 25 | 26 | 27 | 28 | 29 | 30 | 31 |
| Due—May | 3 | 4 | 5 | 6 | 7 | 8 | 9 | 10 | 11 | 12 | 13 | 14 | 15 | 16 | 17 | 18 | 19 | 20 | 21 | 22 | 23 | 24 | 25 | 26 | 27 | 28 | 29 | 30 | 31 | June 1 | 2 |
| Bred—Apr. | 1 | 2 | 3 | 4 | 5 | 6 | 7 | 8 | 9 | 10 | 11 | 12 | 13 | 14 | 15 | 16 | 17 | 18 | 19 | 20 | 21 | 22 | 23 | 24 | 25 | 26 | 27 | 28 | 29 | 30 | |
| Due—June | 3 | 4 | 5 | 6 | 7 | 8 | 9 | 10 | 11 | 12 | 13 | 14 | 15 | 16 | 17 | 18 | 19 | 20 | 21 | 22 | 23 | 24 | 25 | 26 | 27 | 28 | 29 | 30 | July 1 | 2 | |
| Bred—May | 1 | 2 | 3 | 4 | 5 | 6 | 7 | 8 | 9 | 10 | 11 | 12 | 13 | 14 | 15 | 16 | 17 | 18 | 19 | 20 | 21 | 22 | 23 | 24 | 25 | 26 | 27 | 28 | 29 | 30 | 31 |
| Due—July | 3 | 4 | 5 | 6 | 7 | 8 | 9 | 10 | 11 | 12 | 13 | 14 | 15 | 16 | 17 | 18 | 19 | 20 | 21 | 22 | 23 | 24 | 25 | 26 | 27 | 28 | 29 | 30 | 31 | August 1 | 2 |
| Bred—June | 1 | 2 | 3 | 4 | 5 | 6 | 7 | 8 | 9 | 10 | 11 | 12 | 13 | 14 | 15 | 16 | 17 | 18 | 19 | 20 | 21 | 22 | 23 | 24 | 25 | 26 | 27 | 28 | 29 | 30 | |
| Due—August | 3 | 4 | 5 | 6 | 7 | 8 | 9 | 10 | 11 | 12 | 13 | 14 | 15 | 16 | 17 | 18 | 19 | 20 | 21 | 22 | 23 | 24 | 25 | 26 | 27 | 28 | 29 | 30 | 31 | Sept. 1 | |
| Bred—July | 1 | 2 | 3 | 4 | 5 | 6 | 7 | 8 | 9 | 10 | 11 | 12 | 13 | 14 | 15 | 16 | 17 | 18 | 19 | 20 | 21 | 22 | 23 | 24 | 25 | 26 | 27 | 28 | 29 | 30 | 31 |
| Due—September | 2 | 3 | 4 | 5 | 6 | 7 | 8 | 9 | 10 | 11 | 12 | 13 | 14 | 15 | 16 | 17 | 18 | 19 | 20 | 21 | 22 | 23 | 24 | 25 | 26 | 27 | 28 | 29 | 30 | Oct. 1 | 2 |
| Hred—Aug. | 1 | 2 | 3 | 4 | 5 | 6 | 7 | 8 | 9 | 10 | 11 | 12 | 13 | 14 | 15 | 16 | 17 | 18 | 19 | 20 | 21 | 22 | 23 | 24 | 25 | 26 | 27 | 28 | 29 | 30 | 31 |
| Due—October | 3 | 4 | 5 | 6 | 7 | 8 | 9 | 10 | 11 | 12 | 13 | 14 | 15 | 16 | 17 | 18 | 19 | 20 | 21 | 22 | 23 | 24 | 25 | 26 | 27 | 28 | 29 | 30 | 31 | Nov. 1 | 2 |
| Bred—Sept. | 1 | 2 | 3 | 4 | 5 | 6 | 7 | 8 | 9 | 10 | 11 | 12 | 13 | 14 | 15 | 16 | 17 | 18 | 19 | 20 | 21 | 22 | 23 | 24 | 25 | 26 | 27 | 28 | 29 | 30 | |
| Due—November | 3 | 4 | 5 | 6 | 7 | 8 | 9 | 10 | 11 | 12 | 13 | 14 | 15 | 16 | 17 | 18 | 19 | 20 | 21 | 22 | 23 | 24 | 25 | 26 | 27 | 28 | 29 | 30 | Dec. 1 | 2 | |
| Bred—Oct. | 1 | 2 | 3 | 4 | 5 | 6 | 7 | 8 | 9 | 10 | 11 | 12 | 13 | 14 | 15 | 16 | 17 | 18 | 19 | 20 | 21 | 22 | 23 | 24 | 25 | 26 | 27 | 28 | 29 | 30 | 31 |
| Due—December | 3 | 4 | 5 | 6 | 7 | 8 | 9 | 10 | 11 | 12 | 13 | 14 | 15 | 16 | 17 | 18 | 19 | 20 | 21 | 22 | 23 | 24 | 25 | 26 | 27 | 28 | 29 | 30 | 31 | Jan. 1 | 2 |
| Bred—Nov. | 1 | 2 | 3 | 4 | 5 | 6 | 7 | 8 | 9 | 10 | 11 | 12 | 13 | 14 | 15 | 16 | 17 | 18 | 19 | 20 | 21 | 22 | 23 | 24 | 25 | 26 | 27 | 28 | 29 | 30 | |
| Due—January | 3 | 4 | 5 | 6 | 7 | 8 | 9 | 10 | 11 | 12 | 13 | 14 | 15 | 16 | 17 | 18 | 19 | 20 | 21 | 22 | 23 | 24 | 25 | 26 | 27 | 28 | 29 | 30 | 31 | Feb. 1 | |
| Bred—Dec. | 1 | 2 | 3 | 4 | 5 | 6 | 7 | 8 | 9 | 10 | 11 | 12 | 13 | 14 | 15 | 16 | 17 | 18 | 19 | 20 | 21 | 22 | 23 | 24 | 25 | 26 | 27 | 28 | 29 | 30 | 31 |
| Due—February | 2 | 3 | 4 | 5 | 6 | 7 | 8 | 9 | 10 | 11 | 12 | 13 | 14 | 15 | 16 | 17 | 18 | 19 | 20 | 21 | 22 | 23 | 24 | 25 | 26 | 27 | 28 | March 1 | 2 | 3 | 4 |

# Breeding

As the owner of a purebred dog, you may have considered breeding your pet at one time or another. If your dog is a beloved family pet, and not a show dog, you should *not* breed your dog. Breeding is not a hobby for pet owners, but rather a demanding, complicated vocation that is not to be dabbled with. Many people have thought of breeding as an easy-money opportunity: buy two dogs and let them do the work. The rule of thumb is: if you're making money by breeding dogs, you're doing something wrong!

Consider the time and money involved just to get your bitch into breeding condition and then to sustain her throughout pregnancy and afterwards while she tends her young. You will be obligated to house, feed, groom, and housebreak the puppies until good homes can be found for them; and, lest we forget, there will be periodic trips to the vet for check-ups, wormings, and inoculations. Common sense should tell you that it is indeed cruel to bring unwanted or unplanned puppies into an already crowded canine world; only negligent pet owners allow this to happen. Recognizing the number of dogs, purebred and mixed breeds, pet-, show- and breeding-quality, that are put to sleep annually, responsible breeders require that all pet animals be neutered. This condition most often is incorporated into the selling contract. The motives of good breeders are clear: avoid the manufacturing and mass-producing of average and below-average dogs; control the overblown canine population; concentrate on the improvement of purebred bloodlines. Breeding is a noble calling and unless you can improve the breed, you should not consider breeding your animal. Despite all of the obvious virtues of breeding texts, no book could ever prepare a person for breeding. What a heart-breaking and tragic experience to lose an entire litter because a good-intentioned pet owner wasn't aware of potential genetic complications, didn't recognize a breech birth, or couldn't identify the signals of a struggling bitch! Possibly the dam could be lost as well!

Before you take any step towards mating your bitch, think carefully about why you want her to give birth to a litter of puppies. If you feel she will be deprived in some way if she is not bred, if you think your children will learn from the experience, if you have the mistaken notion that you will make money from this great undertaking, think again. A dog can lead a perfectly happy, healthy, normal life without having been mated; in fact, spaying a female and neutering a male helps them become better, longer-lived pets, as they are not so anxious to search for a mate in an effort to relieve their sexual tensions and have a diminished risk of cancer. As for giving the children a lesson in sex education, this is hardly a valid reason for breeding your dog. And on an economic level, it takes not only years of hard work (researching pedigrees and bloodlines, studying genetics, among other things), but it takes plenty of capital (money, equipment, facilities) to make a decent profit from dog breeding.

Why most dedicated breeders are lucky just to break even. If you have only a casual interest in dog breeding, it is best to leave this pastime to those who are more experienced in such matters, those who consider it a serious hobby and a real vocation. If you have bought a breeder– or show-quality canine, one that may be capable of producing champions, and if you are just starting out with this breeding venture, seek advice from the seller of your dog, from

*Breeding dogs requires more than book knowledge. In dogs, breech presentation is not uncommon and the breeder must be prepared to handle this situation and guide the puppy so that neither the pup nor the bitch is injured.*

other veteran breeders, and from your veterinarian before you begin.

The following sections on reproduction are intended for academic value only. This is not a "How-to" chapter on breeding, nor a step-by-step approach for the novice for getting started. Hopefully the reader will understand the depth and complexity of breeding as well as the expected ethical and moral obligations of persons who choose to do so—and never attempt it.

## THE FEMALE "IN SEASON"

A bitch may come into season (also known as "heat" or estrus) once or several times a year, depending on the particular breed and the individual dog. Her first seasonal period, that is to say, the time when she is capable of being fertilized by a male dog, may occur as early as six months with some breeds. If you own a female and your intention is *not* to breed her, by all means discuss with the vet the possibility of having her spayed: this means before she

*Ideally the puppy will be delivered in the normal, head-first position.*

155

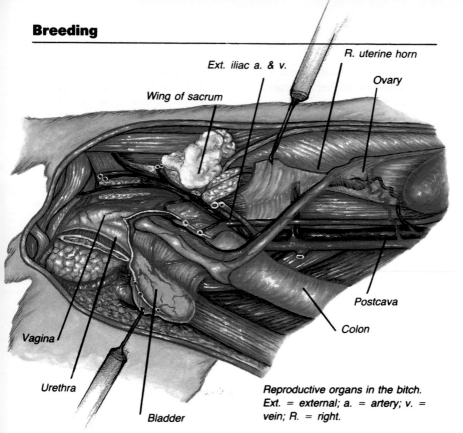

Ext. iliac a. & v.

R. uterine horn

Ovary

Wing of sacrum

Postcava

Colon

Vagina

Urethra

Bladder

Reproductive organs in the bitch.
Ext. = external; a. = artery; v. =
vein; R. = right.

*The reproductive system of the female dog consists of a highly specialized system of organs situated to the rear of the animal.*

reaches sexual maturity.

The first sign of the female's being in season is a thin red discharge, which may increase for about a week; it then changes color to a thin yellowish stain, which lasts about another week. Simultaneously, there is a swelling of the vulva, the exterior portion of the female's reproductive tract; the soft, flabby vulva indicates her readiness to mate. Around this second week or so ovulation

occurs, and this is the crucial period for her to be bred, if this is what you have in mind for her. It is during this middle phase of the heat cycle when conception can take place. Just remember that there is great variation from bitch to bitch with regard to how often they come into heat, how long the heat cycles last, how long the period of ovulation lasts, and how much time elapses between heat cycles. Generally, after the third week of heat, the vulval swelling decreases and the estrus period ceases for several months.

It should be mentioned that the female will probably lose her puppy coat, or at least shed part of it, about three months after she has come into season. This is the time when her puppies would have been weaned, had she been mated, and females generally drop coat at this time.

With female dogs, there are few, if any, behavioral changes during estrus. A bitch may dart out of an open door to greet all available male dogs that show an interest in her, and she may occasionally raise her tail and assume a mating stance, particularly if you pet her lower back; but these signs are not as dramatic as those of the sexually mature male. He himself does

*Each egg within the female is surrounded by a wall that normally takes many sperm to penetrate. In this way, it is more likely that only the strongest sperm will fertilize the egg. A fertile female in season usually has a number of eggs, known as gametes.*

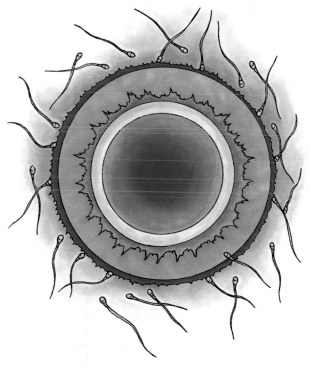

not experience heat cycles; rather, he is attracted to the female during all phases of her seasonal period. He usually becomes more aggressive and tends to fight with other males, especially over females in heat. He tends to mark his territory with urine to attract females and at the same time to warn other competitive males. It is not uncommon to see him mount various objects, and people, in an effort to satisfy his mature sexual urges.

If you are a homeowner and you have an absolutely climb-proof and dig-proof run within your yard, it may be safe to leave your bitch in season there. But then again it may not be a wise idea, as there have been cases of males mating with females right through chain-link fencing! Just to be on the safe side, shut her indoors during her heat periods and don't let her outdoors until you are certain the estrus period is over. Never leave a bitch in heat outdoors, unsupervised, even for a minute so that she can defecate or urinate. If you want to prevent the neighborhood dogs from hanging around your doorstep, as they inevitably will do when they discover your female is in season, take her some distance away from the house before you let her do her business. Otherwise, these canine suitors will be attracted to her by the

arousing odor of her urine, and they will know instinctively that she isn't far from her scented "calling card." If you need to walk your bitch, take her in the car to a nearby park or field for a chance to stretch her legs. Remember that after about three weeks, and this varies from dog to dog, you can let her outdoors again with no worry that she can have puppies until the next heat period.

If you are seriously considering breeding your dog, first talk to as many experienced breeders as possible and read up on the subject in specific books and articles. Only when you are fully aware of the demands and responsibilities of breeding should you make your final decision. It must be stated here that there is no shortage of fine dogs in need of good homes, nor is there likely to be in the foreseeable future. So, if your object in breeding is merely to produce more dogs, you are strongly encouraged to reconsider your objective.

## WHEN TO BREED

It is usually best to breed a bitch when she comes into her second or third season. Plan in advance the time of year which is best for you, taking into account your own schedule of activities (vacations, business trips, social engagements, and so on). Make sure you will be able to set aside

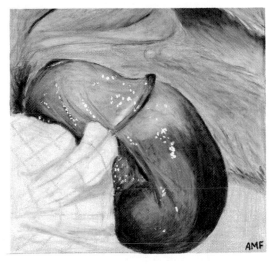

*Each puppy is delivered in a separate membranous sac. This sac must be removed by the bitch without delay—if not, the breeder must come immediately to the assistance of the pup.*

AMF

places are warm and dry). An unused room, such as a dimly lit spare bedroom, can also serve as the place for delivery. If the weather is warm, a large outdoor dog house will do, as long as it is well protected from rain, drafts, and the cold—and enclosed by fencing or a run. A whelping box serves to separate mother and puppies from visitors and other distractions. The walls should be high enough to restrain the puppies yet low enough to allow the mother to take a short respite from her brood after she has fed them. Four feet square is minimum size (for most dogs) and six-to-eight-inch high walls will keep the pups in until they begin to climb; then side walls should be built up so that the young ones cannot wander away from their nest. As the puppies

grow, they really need more room anyway, so double the space with a very low partition down the middle of the box, and soon you will find them naturally housebreaking themselves. Puppies rarely relieve themselves where they sleep. Layers of newspapers spread over the whole area will make excellent bedding and be absorbent enough to keep the surface warm and dry. These should be removed daily and replaced with another thick layer. An old quilt or washable blanket makes better footing for the nursing puppies than slippery newspaper during the first week; this is also softer for the mother to lie on.

Be prepared for the actual whelping several days in advance. Usually the mother will tear up papers, refuse food, and become restless. These may be false alarms; the real test is her temperature, which will drop to below 100°F (38°C) about twelve hours before whelping. Take her temperature with a rectal thermometer, morning and evening, and usher her to her whelping box when her temperature goes down. Keep a close watch on her and make sure she stays safely indoors (or outdoors in a safe enclosure); if she is let outside, unleashed, or allowed to roam freely, she could wander off and start to go into labor. It is possible that she could whelp anywhere, and this could be unfortunate if she needs your assistance.

## WHELPING

Usually little help is needed from you, but it is wise to stay close to be sure that the mother's lack of experience (if this is her first time) does not cause an unnecessary complication. Be ready to help when the first puppy arrives, for it could smother if she does not break the amniotic membrane enclosing it. She should tear open the sac and start licking the puppy, drying and stimulating it. Check to see that all fluids have been cleared from the pup's nostrils and mouth after the mother has licked her youngster clean; otherwise the pup may have difficulty breathing. If the mother fails to tear open the sac and stimulate the newborn's breathing, you can do this yourself by tearing the sack with your hands and then gently rubbing the infant with a soft, rough towel. The afterbirth attached to the puppy by the long umbilical cord, should follow the birth of each puppy. Watch to be sure that each afterbirth is expelled, for the retention of this material can cause infection. In her instinct for cleanliness the mother will probably eat the afterbirth after severing the umbilical cord. One or two meals of this will not hurt her; they stimulate her milk supply, as well as labor, for remaining pups. However, eating too many afterbirths can make her lose appetite for the food she needs to feed her pups and regain her strength. So remove the rest of them, along with the wet newspapers, and keep the box dry and clean.

If the mother does not bite the cord or bites it too close to the puppy's body, take over the job to prevent an umbilical hernia. Tearing is recommended, but you can cut the cord, about two inches from the body, with a sawing motion with scissors that have been sterilized in alcohol. Then dip the end of the cut cord in a shallow dish of iodine; the cord will dry up and fall off in a few days.

The puppies should follow

youngsters, but don't take them out of her sight. Let her handle things if your interference seems to make her nervous.

Be sure that all the puppies are getting enough to eat. If the mother sits or stands instead of lying still to nurse, the probable cause is scratching from the puppies' nails. You can remedy this by clipping them, as you would the bitch's, with a pet nail clipper. Manicure scissors also do

furnished with a heating pad and/or heating lamp and some bedding material. Leave half the litter with the mother and the other half in the extra box, changing off at two-hour intervals at first. Later you may exchange them less frequently, leaving them all together except during the day. Try supplementary feedings, too. As soon as their eyes open, at about two weeks, they will lap from a small dish.

*"Pooping" the puppies, or rubbing the bowels and genitals to stimulate elimination, may be necessary if the bitch doesn't tend to this herself.*

for these tiny claws. Some breeders advise disposing of the smaller or weaker pups in a large litter, as the mother has trouble handling more than six or seven. You can help her out by preparing an extra puppy box or basket

## WEANING THE PUPPIES

Normally the puppies should be completely weaned at five weeks, although you can start to feed them at three weeks. They will find it easier to lap semi-solid food than to drink milk at first, so

# Breeding

mix baby cereal with whole or evaporated milk, warmed to body temperature, and offer it to the puppies in a saucer. Until they learn to lap it, it is best to feed one or two at a time because they are more likely to walk into it than to eat it. Hold the saucer at their chin level, and let them gather around, keeping paws off the dish. Cleaning with a damp sponge afterward prevents most of the cereal from sticking to the pups if the mother doesn't clean them up. Once they have gotten the idea, broth or babies' meat soup may be alternated with milk, and you can start them on finely chopped meat. At about four weeks, they will eat four meals a day and soon do without their mother entirely. Start them on canned dog food, or leave dry puppy food with them in a dish

for self-feeding. Don't leave the water dish with them all the time; at this age everything is a play toy and they will use it as a wading pool. They can drink all they need if it is offered several times a day, after meals. As the puppies grow up, the mother will go into their "pen" only to nurse them, first sitting up and then standing. To dry up her milk

*All puppies are susceptible to worms. Deworming must begin at a very early age with the supervision of a professional.*

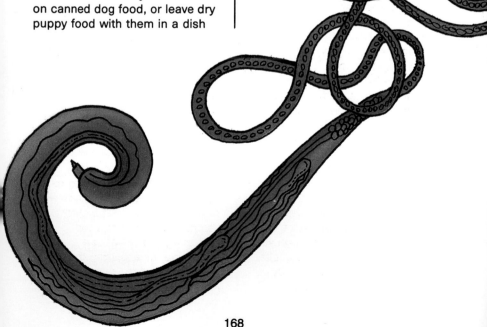

*Bottle-feeding may be necessary with particularly large litters or with a bitch who has become overly stressed or neglectful.*

supply completely, keep the mother away for longer periods; after a few days of part-time nursing she can stay away for even longer periods, and then permanently. The little milk left will be resorbed by her body.

The puppies may be put outside during the day, unless it is too cold or rainy, as soon as their eyes are open. They will benefit from the sunlight. A rubber mat or newspapers underneath will protect them from cold or dampness. As they mature, the pups can be let out for longer intervals, although you must provide them with a shelter at night or in bad weather. By now, cleaning up after the

matured youngsters is a man-sized job, so put them out at least during the day and make your task easier. If you enclose them in a run or kennel, remember to clean it *daily*, as various parasites and other infectious organisms may be lurking if the quarters are kept dirty.

You can expect the pups to need at least one worming before they are ready to go to new homes. Before the pups are three weeks old, take a stool sample from each to your veterinarian. The vet can determine, by analyzing the stool, if any of the pups have worms—and if so, what kind of worms are present. If one puppy is infected, then all should be wormed as a preventive measure. Follow the veterinarian's advice; this also applies to vaccinations. You will want to vaccinate the pups at the earliest possible age. This way, the pups destined for new homes will be protected against some of the more debilitating canine diseases.

## THE DECISION TO SPAY OR NEUTER

If you decide not to use your male or female for breeding, or if you are obligated to have the animal altered based on an agreement made between you and the seller, make the

necessary arrangements with your veterinarian as soon as possible. The surgery involved for both males and females is relatively simple and painless: males will be castrated and females will have their ovaries and uterus removed. In both cases, the operation does not alter their personalities; you will, however, notice that males will be less likely to roam, to get into fights with other male dogs, and to mount objects and people.

Your veterinarian can best determine at what age neutering or spaying should be done. With a young female dog, the operation may be somewhat more involved, and as a result be more costly; however, in the long

*The breeder must actively partake in cleaning the pup after feedings. Hands-on contact serves as the initial step in socialization—accustoming the pup to his human family.*

| PUPPY GROWTH AND BREEDER RESPONSIBILITY | |
|---|---|
| **AGE** | **REQUIRED CARE/EXPECTED DEVELOPMENT** |
| WEEKS 1–2 | Helpless; dam must provide constant care; owner must ensure warmth and cleanliness; puppy nurses, crawls, needs stimulation for elimination; sleeps 90% of time. |
| WEEKS 3–4 | Owner sustains optimum environment; puppy is alert, laps from bowl, takes first steps; defecates on its own; baby teeth emerge; barks, wags tail. |
| WEEKS 4–5 | Ambles, growls, and bites; play and interaction increase; human contact limited but essential; learning begins. |
| WEEKS 5–6 | Weaning; human socialization vital; pack order apparent; sex play; explores and sleeps less. |
| WEEKS 6–8 | Two to three daily meals; puppy accustomed to human family; breeder initiates housetraining; first veterinary visit; wary of the unknown. |

run you will be glad you made the decision to have this done for your pet. After a night or two at the veterinarian's or an animal hospital, your bitch can be safely returned to your home. Her stitches will heal in a short time, and when they are removed, you will hardly notice her souvenir scar of the routine operation. Once she has been spayed, she no longer will be capable of having a litter of puppies.

Check with your city or town or with the local humane society for special programs that are available for pet owners. In many municipalities you can have your pet altered for just a small fee; the low price is meant to encourage pet owners to take advantage of this important means of birth control for their dogs. Pet adoption agencies and other animal welfare organizations can house only so many animals at one time, given the money, space, and other resources they have available. This is why pet owners are urged to have their pets altered, so that puppies resulting from accidental breedings won't end up being put to sleep as so many others have that are lost, stray, unwanted, or abandoned.

# Dogs and the Law

BY ANMARIE BARRIE

No matter where you live, there will be laws and ordinances restricting the ownership of pets— exotic and wild animals (such as monkeys, pythons, and ocelots) as well as the more traditionally kept domestics (such as dogs and cats). This chapter purports to investigate with brevity the laws which pertain to the ownership and keeping of the domestic canine. Like all other things, laws change and evolve over time, and vary from locale to locale. The information supplied in this chapter is meant as a general guideline for the dog owner. Every owner is strongly encouraged to contact his local authorities to keep abreast on new laws and amendments to existing laws so that he can be the most responsible owner possible.

## BUYING AND SELLING

Certain specific laws apply to the purchasing and peddling of pooches. Laws in these areas grow ever more stringent, so the potential buyer and/or seller is well advised to be aware of the laws pertaining to his transactions where dogs are concerned. Dealers and breeders, in most instances, are treated differently from the average dog owner who is trying to sell his first litter. Regardless, a sales contract is in order, a written agreement outlining the various dimensions of the sale. Sales contracts may indicate the quality of the dog, i.e.,

the pet-quality, show-quality, breeder-quality; the sex of the dog; and the breed of the dog. In addition to these basic essentials, the specifics, as registered with the national kennel club, should be included, i.e., the names and registration numbers of the sire and dam; the litter registration number; addresses of all involved, etc. Warranties and conditions of the sale should also be expressly stated, and no implications or unexpressed conditions may apply. For instance, the return policy, the guaranteed pedigree of the dog, the health of the dog (including the possibility of congenital defects in later years) should all be addressed. Replacement warranties are also appropriate to include, should something happen to the purchased puppy. Should a given puppy (of intended show-quality) begin to exhibit faults disqualified in the breed standard, the buyer is able to return the dog. Commonly, if the seller is no longer in the business of selling dogs, the buyer is entitled to half of the agreed-upon price.

## GENERAL GUIDELINES FOR DOG OWNERS

"Give to God what is God's, give to Caesar what is Caesar's" is a Gospel quote that has been used and manipulated since it was originally uttered two thousand years ago. The concept of paying taxes has never sat well with humans, nor does it sit well with dogs. Licenses are basically taxes on dogs, though as pet owners we need not stew over the unfairness of "yet another tax." The purpose of licensing dogs is a valid and important one. Licenses serve as a positive means of identifying an animal and afford an owner with a fair chance of regaining his dog if lost or stolen. Licenses also provide a dog additional consideration by authorities and even from strangers, who will respect the fact the owner of this dog cares enough to identify it and affix its ID to its collar.

Many owners resist the call to license their dogs on the premise that their dogs are house dogs or yard dogs, or never ever walk off their leashes. Nonetheless, accidents and mishaps occur regularly, and it's better to be safe than sorry (why not be safe and law-abiding!?). The threat of impoundment and the treatment which dogs receive as a matter of course from such authorities should be scare tactic enough to persuade an owner to license his dog.

The cost of licenses varies from place to place as well as from dog to dog. Licenses for assistance dogs, such as Seeing Eye dogs, hearing dogs, or any handicap-assistance dogs, may be substan-

# Dogs and the Law

tially less than a regular dog. In some areas, assistance dogs receive their licenses gratis, or are covered by their training agency. Recognizing the growing problem of dog over-population, many towns and cities offer reduced license fees for spayed and neutered dogs.

Vaccinations for dogs deserve special mention. Depending on where you live, the vaccination for rabies may or may not be mandatory. In some places, this vaccination is optional. While the chances of your well-kept canine acquiring rabies today may be minuscule, the cases are not so isolated and unheard of that an owner can rest in ultimate confidence. Generally a vaccinated dog can avoid being

quarantined in the unfortunate event that it should bite a stranger or would-be assailant. The age for vaccination varies, but most usual is six months old. If a puppy is under the age of six months, it is advisable not to permit it to socialize with unknown dogs on the street. Keep in mind that vaccinations need to be kept updated for both rabies and other diseases.

Among the most common-sense concerns of current-day owners are leash laws. Responsible dog owners marvel with dismay over dogs which run the neighborhood without a collar, supervision, or their owner's concern. Caring dog proprietors are grateful for leash laws as it is the protection of the dog, as well as human passers-by, that is concerned. That a dog is under control at all times remains the premise of leash laws. Dogs that are given the "freedom" to wander the neighborhood or city block are likewise given the "right" to be impounded, snatched and/or injured. Fines are often issued against owners who do not abide by the leash laws of their community.

Running hand in hand, or paw in paw, with leash laws are muzzle ordinances. These laws require

that a dog be muzzled at all times when it is in public. Although these laws are less commonplace than leash laws, they do exist in certain communities. Owners are advised to investigate if muzzle laws apply in their area.

Pooper-scooper laws are being enforced in more and more areas these days. "Curb Your Dog" signs have become as common as pedestrian crossings and "Yield signs." For the cleanliness of our communities, these kinds of laws are invented; in order to do our part as responsible dog owners and citizens, we must abide by these clean-up rules. While persons who live in the country have more gripes with these laws, city dwellers fully understand the need to observe these ordinances. Scoops are sold in pet shops, or you can employ simple plastic bags. It is assured that if you are the person walking behind the behind of a 250-pound pooch, you will be grateful for these laws. Some owners use brown paper sheets or newspapers (preferably yesterday's) to assist in the clean-up.

Anti-cruelty laws are geared towards the protection of animals on the whole, sparing dogs from potential, often unintentional, abuse. Laws such as these are sweeping the nations, as an increasing number of people become aware of deleterious situations arising for all animals. While active cruelty to an animal evokes rage in any human being, there are more subtle displays of cruelty which these laws attempt to pinpoint—cruelty in the form of neglect and careless treatment. Persons who are found in violation of anti-cruelty laws are very often subject to fines. All citizens are encouraged to report any cases of cruelty which they witness or suspect to be happening. Commonly, ordinances prohibit the keeping of a dog in a parked car, which can be a cruel, irresponsible practice in most situations. Dogs have been known to suffer from heat prostration, and worse.

Anti-cruelty laws have also seeped into the world of puppy mills, as more and more of these

175

# Dogs and the Law

unethical outfits are being undermined by concerned owners. The cruel treatment of animals in these farms must be combated by increased legislation. Always know the source of your potential new dog. Avoid sellers who cannot give you all the answers you want to know.

As heart-breaking and unimaginable as it seems, our dogs are not permitted in a great number of places. "No Dog" signs are frequently posted in buildings, parks, restaurants, motels, etc. It seems that dogs are more accepted in Continental countries, where dogs are permitted (even invited) to dine with the family at a fine restaurant. This not being the case in every American state or city of Great Britain, law-abiding citizens must contend with these restrictions.

Ordinances involving the number of dogs which an owner can keep are prevalent in most communities. These laws vary from place to place and from residency to residency. Whether you live in an apartment, condominium, house, or farm, there may be laws regulating the number of pets you are able to keep. Homes that wish to keep more than the maximum number of animals may be forced to apply for a kennel license or be subject to a daily fine and regular inspection.

For sake of neighbors and the general health of your family, it is wise to take these restrictions to heart. No matter how great your love of animals is, it is not humane to the animals involved to subject them to over-crowding and minimal attention. A small suburban apartment can quickly become the haven of 75 stray dogs and cats, should the owner so choose. Laws such as these prohibit these kinds of communes from blossoming all over the nation.

In most well-organized communities, there are organizations that specialize in Lost and Found dogs. For your dog's safety, you must have the dog licensed and vaccinated, as dogs that are protected in this way have a greater chance of finding their way back home, unscathed. If you have lost your dog, do not panic, but do work fast. The more people to whom you speak and angles that you take, the greater your chances of retrieving your lost pet. All local authorities (police, fire company, animal control organizations) and all types of media organizations (radio, newspapers, town crier) should be commissioned to lend a hand, keep out a keen eye and ear for the lost dog. Advertising through posters, newspapers, radio, and community lists will pay off in the end. Written descriptions, accompanied by photographs, can assist in helping people have a better mental image of the dog.

Prevention can never be overstressed. Licensing is a must, and the dog must wear the ID tag. Tattoos are quick becoming very popular. These should be located on the dog's inner thigh, not on its ear, as that appendage can easily be torn off by a thief. Tattoos have

worked for generations on pack dogs, and the same philosophy of identification can work for pet owners too. Often, the dog's kennel club number or other identifying number is tattooed onto the dog.

Impoundment threatens lost dogs and all other dogs running at large, particularly those without collars and licenses. Most animal control authorities maintain the right to impound, sell, and/or destroy any animal that they catch. As an owner's legal property, a dog cannot be impounded or confiscated without the owner's notice. Of course, if the dog is loose and unidentified, the owner is knowingly waiving his rights, and thereby his chances of seeing that the dog has a fair chance to find its way home. A dog that proves itself a nuisance or dangerous to property and people may be confiscated; the owner may be notified ex post facto. An owner may then be invited to court to defend its dog's right to life.

Pounds, as a rule, are required

to keep a dog for a certain period of time before disposing of it in any permanent way. However, this period rarely exceeds four days in length, so owners must act expediently. The fortunate owner who does find his dog at the pound must have the dog vaccinated and licensed (if not done previously), as well as pay a fine. Unclaimed pets are either destroyed humanely or offered for adoption. Many pounds reserve the right to have the owner spay or neuter his unchained canine.

There are also laws that regard the disposal of a dog's remains. Owners must be aware of restrictions in this area. Under certain legislative bodies, a person is not allowed to bury his dog on his own property. In most cases, contacting your family veterinarian or a humane society to handle the details of burial is the most expeditious approach.

## DOGS AS PROPERTY

Let there be no doubt about it: a dog is the personal property of its owner. This fact is well substantiated in the various legal codes and statutes under which we all live our daily lives. For dog owners, the dog's legal-property status can be considered a mixed blessing. On the one hand, the dog's legal status as property necessarily guarantees the owner certain rights under the law, the very same rights which pertain to the possession of other property. Homeowners especially should be familiar with some of these rights. On the other hand, the dog's status as legal property places very considerable responsibility on the shoulders of the dog owner, for he will be held legally accountable for the actions of his dog—

# Dogs and the Law

just as the homeowner is legally responsible for any injuries that occur on his property and are the result of, for example, negligence resulting from the owner's maintenance of the property.

For the dog owner to be entitled to the rights of a property owner pertinent to his dog, the dog in question must be licensed by the appropriate authorities, usually the local governing body. However, because of the nature of legal systems in most of the free countries, laws may vary from town to town, county to county, and state to state. Thus the owner is strongly encouraged to investigate the necessary requirements for licensing his dog. At the same time, the owner is encouraged to ascertain the exact nature of the rights of a dog owner under the given laws applicable to the given place of residence.

This varying nature of laws makes it impossible for one to offer details on many of the rights and responsibilities of the dog owner. However, regardless of the place of residence, the dog owner is entitled to due process with regard to the taking of the licensed dog. Due process in this regard refers essentially to the necessary notification of the owner before any further action can be taken by the authorities. In

this way, the owner is offered a chance to act on the behalf of his dog, his legal property.

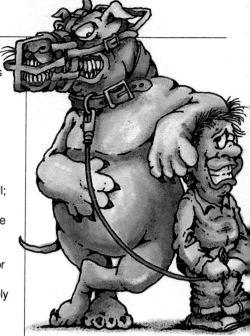

An additional consequence of the legal-property status of the dog is that, as property, the dog cannot be considered a person under the law. One effect of this fact is that the dog therefore cannot be the beneficiary of a will; however, provisions for the care and continued maintenance of the dog can be, and should be, carefully spelled out in the will—just as it would be for the home or any other piece of property.

In summary, the dog is definitely considered property under the law. As such, the dog owner is entitled to given rights and held accountable for given responsibilities. To be granted these rights, the dog owner must license his dog, as well as follow any other guidelines required under the laws of his or her place of residence. Finally, as property, the dog cannot be considered a person, and this fact holds various implications.

Because the dog is the legal property of the dog owner, the dog owner is legally responsible for the behavior of his dog, as well as for the care and maintenance of the animal. However, when the dog is in the possession of a person other than the owner, such as a temporary caretaker, that other person may be held responsible for the dog, depending on the specific circumstances involved and the specific laws of the jurisdiction in which the action(s) occurs. To offer an example, consider the following scenario: A dog is owned by Mr. Smith, who leaves on vacation and hires an individual to care for his dog. While Mr. Smith is on vacation, the dog caretaker walks the dog without a leash and the dog bites a child. Of course, because the dog is property and not person, someone must be held accountable. Should it be Mr. Smith or the caretaker? In such a case it is likely that the caretaker would be held accountable for the dog's biting of the child, provided of course that Mr. Smith did not leave directions to walk the dog without a leash, etc. As we can

# Dogs and the Law

see, many variables can come into play regarding legal responsibility for the dog.

To keep it simple in an attempt to offer the reader as much information as possible without getting weighed down in extraneous details, a few general guidelines will be presented.

First, the dog owner, for all intents and purposes, should raise, train, and keep his dog under the assumption that he is legally responsible for every action and for the entire well-being of his dog, ranging from obeying pooper-scooper laws to anti-cruelty laws to dog-bite statutes. In this way, the owner will act as responsibly as possible and, in the end, avoid possible law suits. Secondly, whenever leaving the dog in the custody of others, whether for a short time or a prolonged period, the dog owner should leave clear, explicit written directions regarding proper and appropriate care of the dog. These directions can be prepared ahead of time and kept on file by the owner for use whenever the need arises. In so doing, the owner protects himself in the case of a lawsuit. Thirdly, a minor can be held legally responsible for the dog as property, and this fact needs to be considered whenever a youngster is in charge of the

dog. Lastly, the dog owner must familiarize himself with the laws that pertain to him as a dog owner, as a resident of his given community. In no other way can the dog owner act responsibly and thus be protected under the law.

Because the dog owner is legally responsible for his dog, he is liable for all damages and personal injuries that result from the dog. Under strict liability, the owner is liable for any damages or injury caused by the dog, even if they are not the "fault" of the owner. Of course, common law doctrines are the products of court decisions, and thus may vary from place to place. Additionally,

liability may be subject to the same circumstantial variables as those which apply to responsibility in general.

Because the owner is liable for the actions of his dog, he can be taken to court and sued. A person injured by a dog will likely receive reimbursement for all medical expenses, as well as a given sum for pain and suffering, depending on the circumstances. The same conditions apply to damages: a person can receive full reimbursement for the loss or damage of any property that was the product of the dog's actions. In serious cases, e.g., those involving blatant negligence, malice or forethought,

# Dogs and the Law

the owner of the dog can be sentenced to prison and/or fined.

The subject of vicious dogs abounds in controversy, in part because of the lack of an all-encompassing definition of viciousness as it pertains to the dog and in part because there is a current trend to label entire breeds of dog as inherently vicious. Because of the controversial nature of the vicious-dog subject, the reader is encouraged to do two things: first, read up on the specific laws pertaining to canine viciousness that apply to his locale; and second, to employ utmost common sense in the execution of his dog-owning responsibilities. The first step is by far the easier of the two, for vicious-dog statutes can be found in most libraries and at many municipal buildings. Beginning with inquiries and following up with research ensures the dog owner expedient acquisition of the applicable laws regarding viciousness and his dog. The second step, regarding the application of common sense to all aspects of canine ownership, requires that the dog owner first obey all laws pertinent to his ownership, e.g., leash laws, proper training, housing, restriction, etc.; second be well aware and understand the nature of his charge and adjust its keeping accordingly; and lastly take all steps necessary to ensure that others who may care for the dog be explicitly instructed on how to execute their caretaker task.

By following the two-step process just described to help you guard against a potential vicious-dog law suit, especially in following the application of common sense to your dog ownership, you to a large degree also work to prevent injury, both to yourself and to others. In so doing, you are also necessarily limiting the possibility that you will find yourself beside your dog in court over your dog's injuring another person.

To assist the dog owner in applying common sense to his dog ownership, the following principles are presented: (1) all dogs, meaning each and every dog, no matter how small or large a dog, young or old a dog, has the potential to injure a person; (2) dogs act largely on instinct and perceive the world much differently than people do, i.e., a dog may see a situation as dangerous and react with fear biting even though a person sees the situation as perfectly non-threatening or even pleasant; (3) not all people are dog fanciers, and some people even delight in provoking and taunting an animal, which can easily lead to their being injured; (4) dogs do not treat all people in the same manner as they treat you, their owner and caretaker.

By considering these principles, obeying the laws of dog ownership (which essentially are designed for the protection of you, your dog, and others), and consis-

tently applying common sense in your daily doggie doings, you by and large prevent injury.

In recent years, insurance companies have offered insurance policies to dog owners. Essentially these policies can be grouped into two general categories: canine life insurance and liability insurance. Of course, many different policies from each category are offered, and the cost of the respective policy varies roughly in accordance with the coverage offered. For example, a "life" insurance policy that covered accidental injury as well as providing a death benefit will typically cost more than a policy that offers only a death benefit, provided of course that the death benefits are of equivalent value.

Canine insurance is not for every dog owner, though every dog owner is encouraged to investigate the various policies offered and for themselves make the determination of whether yea or nay they purchase such insurance. Common consensus offers that canine insurance is best suited for two kinds of dog owners, a splitting that roughly corresponds to the two kinds of canine insurance offered. The first kind of owner is the professional breeder

# Dogs and the Law

and/or showperson, who has invested large sums of money in his individual dogs and stands to lose much in the case of accidental injury or death. Such a person is strongly encouraged to investigate the canine life insurance available. In short, he is encouraged to protect his investment. The second type of person is the owner of a guard dog or any dog trained or demonstrating the proclivity to attack a person. For this dog owner, investigation of some type of liability insurance is encouraged.

After all is said and done, after all steps and measures towards responsible lawful ownership have been taken, there may still come a time when the dog owner finds himself in the midst of a controversy. The cause may be a very simple or insignificant one, or it may be a very complex one. The important point to remember is that a controversy must be managed in a legal and responsible way.

If the controversy is a minor one, it might be best to attempt to resolve the the problem between the two parties, in which case a third party (an objective mediator) often proves helpful. If this fails for any reason, e.g., tempers, then going to the authorities is strongly recommended. In no case should anyone attempt to take matters into their own hands, becoming

judge, jury, and executioner all in one. If the controversy involves a serious matter, you are encouraged to seek legal advice as soon as possible. Remember that you are responsible for the actions of your dog, and therefore you can be held liable for any damages or injuries that your dog may inflict. All controversies should be approached in an objective manner; the dog owner must realize that there are at least two sides to the story and that resolution of the conflict will likely involve at least small compromises from each of the parties involved.

## CRUELTY

What determines or defines cruelty to animals often excites great controversy in our society.

Anti-cruelty legislation, nonetheless, continues to make headway, as new laws are being enforced with regularity. Avoiding the inhumane treatment of animals, neglect and abuse should be the target of all caring dog owners. The conditions of a breeding facility or animal shelter, cosmetic alterations of puppies (cropping ears and docking tails), protocol for dealing with an injured animal, and impoundment of lost, vicious or destructive dogs are just some of the topics which anti-cruelty laws address. In the United States, ear cropping and tail docking are not prohibited as they are in Great Britain. Britain has for generations deemed such cosmetic alterations unnecessary and unnecessarily cruel.

Air travel can be a more difficult matter. Airlines most usually allow dogs to fly on their flights. Small dogs can be carried on, while large ones need to be kept in the baggage area. Of course the appropriate crate is required for any dog traveling by air. Mark the crate: "Live Cargo" or "This End Up" for the safety of your canine luggage. Travel agents are usually well informed and will advise you on such decisions.

## LANDLORDS AND DOGS

Regardless of how it may seem, there is no *natural* antipathy between landlords and dogs. Dogs in themselves are no more the natural enemy of landlords

## TRAVEL

When traveling with your dog, there are a number of considerations with which to be concerned. The most common method of travel is automobiles, though fewer laws address this mode of transportation. Regarding urban travel, i.e., buses, subways, rails, dogs are usually not permitted on board unless the dog is an assistance dog. Some railways allow dogs to stay in the owner's cabin, while others require that the dog be kept in the baggage compartment (likely there is an area especially equipped for live cargo). Always check with the railway and train station about the regulations regarding your dog. Do this before leaving home! If you intend to travel by sea, less common in today's world of airplanes, it is advised that similar inquiries be made to the ship's station.

than, say, tenants are. Landlords and dogs don't get along for the most part because in many cases dogs and tenants—both dog owners and non-dog owners—don't get along. Landlords often try to outlaw the ownership of dogs by their tenants simply because dogs make trouble. They can be destructive, they can make messes, they can scare people, they can hurt people. To avoid the trouble that dogs can make, landlords write into their leases clauses that prohibit the keeping of dogs by tenants. Landlords in general might not be the nicest people in the world, but you can't blame them for wanting to avoid trouble and expense that tenants' pet dogs may bring them. For

example, would you as landlord relish the idea of being sued by some troublemaking yardbird who, while visiting one of your tenants, was bitten by his homicidal cur? And don't ask why he'd be suing the landlord when it wasn't the landlord's dog that bit him—he'd be suing everyone in sight, as the courts encourage that type of madness: wouldn't a reasonably prudent landlord provide 24-hour guard service to make sure that visitors are not attacked in their buildings?

Governmental units at various levels are telling landlords that they can't tell their tenants not to own dogs (or cats), and various courts are starting to tell landlords that either their leases don't say what they plainly do say or that they say it but the courts don't like it and will therefore come up with a reason why it shouldn't be allowed. But the milennium for dog-owning apartment dwellers has not yet arrived; until it does, the best thing a tenant can do is to ask for permission from the owner...and to get it in writing.

# Index

## Dog Breeding for Professionals
By Dr. Herbert Richards (H-969)

For dog owners who need and actively seek good advice about how to go about breeding their dogs whether for profit or purely because of their attachment to animals. *Please note* that the breeding photography is sexually explicit and some readers may find it offensive.

*Hard cover, 5.5 in x 8 in, 224 pages, 105 black and white photos, 62 color photos.*
*ISBN 0-87666-659-4a*

## Dog Training
By Lew Burke (H-962)

The elements of dog training are easy to grasp and apply. The author uses the psychological makeup of dogs to his advantage by making them want to be what they should be—substituting the family for the pack.

*Hard cover, 5.5 in x 8 in, 255 pages, 64 black and white photos, 23 color photos.*
*ISBN 0-87666-656-X*

## The Mini Atlas of Dog Breeds
By Andrew De Prisco & James B. Johnson (H-1106)

An identification handbook giving a concise and thorough look at over 400 of the world's dog breeds. The authors' enthusiastic and knowledgeable approach brings to life instantly man's oldest friend and companion. A flowing and witty text, further enlivened by 500 full-color photos, successfully maps out the world of dogs; an easy-reference format pinpoints each breed's development, portrait, registry, and

pet attributes. The volume is captioned with specially designed symbols.

*Hard cover, 5.5 in x 8.5 in, 544 pages, nearly 700 color photos.*
*ISBN 0-86622-091-7*

## Dog Owner's Encyclopedia of Veterinary Medicine
By Allan H. Hart, B.V.Sc. (H-934)

Written by a vet who feels that most dog owners should recognize the symptoms and understand the cures of most diseases of dogs so they can properly communicate with their veterinarian. This book is a necessity for every dog owner, especially those who have more than one dog. *Hard cover, 5.5 in x 8 in, 186 pages, 86 black and white photos. ISBN 0-87666-287-4*

### The Proper Care of Dogs
By Christopher Burris (TW-102)
Discusses the basic care of all dogs and highlights the specific needs of every A.K.C.—recog-

nized breed. Ideal for the prospective dog owner, this compact and colorful book lays the groundwork for general canine management and provides an overview of the world of dogs. *Hard cover, 5 in x 7 in, 256 pages, over 200 full-color photos. ISBN 0-86622-402-5*

### The Atlas of Dog Breeds of the World
By Bonnie Wilcox, DVM, & Chris Walkowicz (H-1091)
Traces the history and highlights the characteristics, appearance and function of every recognized dog breed in the world. 409 different breeds receive full-color treatment and individual study. Hundreds of breeds in addition to those recognized by the American Kennel Club and the Kennel Club of Great Britain are included—the dogs of the world complete! The ultimate reference work, comprehensive coverage, intelligent and delightful discussions. The perfect gift book. *Hard cover, 9 in x 12 in, 912 pages, 1,106 color photos. ISBN 0-86622-930-2*

The **ATLAS** of **DOG BREEDS** of the World (t.f.h.)

**NEW! THIRD EDITION** With 100 **NEW** color photos

BONNIE WILCOX, DVM, —and— CHRIS WALKOWICZ

**OVER 1100 FULL-COLOR PHOTOS**

The most comprehensive fully illustrated volume on dogs ever published--- *EVERY* photo in full color